Robert Rose's Favorite

SOUPS & STEWS

Robert
ROSE

ROBERT ROSE'S FAVORITE SOUPS AND STEWS

Copyright © 1998 Robert Rose Inc.

Canadian Cataloguing in Publication Data

Main entry under title:

Robert Rose's favorite soups and stews

Includes index.

ISBN 1-896503-69-1

1. Soups.   2. Stews   I. Title: Favorite soups & stews.
III. Title: Robert Rose's favorite soups and stews.

TX757.R62 1998   641.8'13   C98-931528-2

DESIGN AND PAGE COMPOSITION: MATTHEWS COMMUNICATIONS DESIGN '
PHOTOGRAPHY: MARK T. SHAPIRO

Cover photo: (AVOCADO SOUP, PAGE 14)

Distributed in the U.S. by: Distributed in Canada by:
Firefly Books (U.S.) Inc.   Stoddart Publishing Co. Ltd.
P.O. Box 1338   34 Lesmill Road
Ellicott Station   North York, Ontario
Buffalo, NY   14205   M3B 2T6

ORDER LINES   ORDER LINES
Tel: (416) 499-8412   Tel: (416) 445-3333
Fax: (416) 499-8313   Fax: (416) 445-5967

Published by: Robert Rose Inc. • 156 Duncan Mill Road, Suite 12
Toronto, Ontario, Canada M3B 2N2   Tel: (416) 449-3535

Printed in Canada   1234567 BP 01 00 99 98

About this book

At Robert Rose, we're committed to finding imaginative and exciting ways to provide our readers with cookbooks that offer great recipes — and exceptional value. That's the thinking behind our "Robert Rose's Favorite" series.

Here we've selected over 50 favorite soup and stew recipes from a number of our best-selling full-sized cookbooks: Byron Ayanoglu's *New Vegetarian Gourmet* and *Simply Mediterranean Cooking*; Johanna Burkhard's *Comfort Food Cookbook*; Andrew Chase's *Asian Bistro Cookbook*; *New World Noodles* and *New World Chinese Cooking*, by Bill Jones and Stephen Wong; and Rose Reisman's *Light Cooking, Light Pasta, Enlightened Home Cooking* and *Light Vegetarian Cooking*.

We believe that it all adds up to great value for anyone who loves soups and stews.

Want to find out more about the sources of our recipes? See pages 95 and 96 for details.

Contents

Hot Soups

Cold Soups

Meat Stews

Fish and Seafood Stews

Vegetable Stews

Hot Soups

Serves 6

Creamy Tomato Soup

A sunny window sill may seem like the ideal place to ripen tomatoes, but hot blistering sun can end up baking them instead. To ripen, place tomatoes in a paper bag and leave on the counter at room temperature. Never store tomatoes in the fridge; it numbs their delicate flavor.

I always look forward to late summer — when baskets of lush ripe tomatoes are the showpiece in outdoor markets — so I can make this silky smooth soup. In winter, vine-ripened greenhouse tomatoes make a good stand-in, particularly if you use a little tomato paste for extra depth. Just add 1 to 2 tbsp (15 to 25 mL) when puréeing soup.

FROM
The Comfort Food Cookbook
by Johanna Burkhard

PREHEAT OVEN TO 400° F (200° C)

1 tbsp	olive oil	15 mL
6	ripe tomatoes (2 lbs [1 kg]), cored and quartered	6
1	medium leek, white and light green part only, chopped	1
1	small onion, coarsely chopped	1
2	medium carrots, peeled and coarsely chopped	2
1	stalk celery including leaves, chopped	1
2	large cloves garlic, sliced	2
1/2 tsp	salt	2 mL
1/4 tsp	pepper	1 mL
Pinch	nutmeg	Pinch
3 cups	chicken stock *or* vegetable stock (approximate)	750 mL
1 cup	light (15%) cream	250 mL
2 tbsp	chopped fresh herbs such as parsley, basil or chives	25 mL

1. Drizzle oil over bottom of a large shallow roasting pan. Add tomatoes, leek, onion, carrot, celery and garlic; season with salt, pepper and nutmeg.

2. Roast, uncovered, in preheated oven, stirring often, for 1 1/4 hours or until vegetables are very tender, but not brown.

3. Add 2 cups (500 mL) of the stock to pan; purée mixture in batches, preferably in a blender or a food processor, until very smooth. Strain soup through a sieve into large saucepan.

4. Add cream and enough of the remaining stock to thin soup to desired consistency. Adjust seasoning with salt and pepper to taste. Heat until piping hot; do not let the soup boil or it may curdle. Ladle into warm bowls; sprinkle with fresh herbs.

Serves 4 to 6

Cauliflower Potato Soup

TIP

Buy cauliflower with bright, light-colored heads and tightly packed florets.

For a stronger taste, use aged Cheddar or Swiss cheese.

MAKE AHEAD

Prepare and refrigerate up to a day before and reheat before serving, adding more stock if too thick.

1 tbsp	vegetable oil	15 mL
1 tsp	crushed garlic	5 mL
1 cup	chopped onions	250 mL
1	medium cauliflower, separated into florets	1
4 cups	chicken stock	1 L
2	small potatoes, peeled and chopped	2
1/4 cup	shredded Cheddar cheese	50 mL
2 tbsp	chopped fresh chives	25 mL

1. In large nonstick saucepan, heat oil; sauté garlic and onions until softened, approximately 5 minutes.

2. Add cauliflower, stock and potatoes; bring to a boil. Cover, reduce heat and simmer for 25 minutes or until tender. Transfer to food processor and purée until creamy and smooth. Return to saucepan and thin with more stock if desired.

3. Ladle into bowls; sprinkle with cheese and chives.

FROM
Rose Reisman Brings Home Light Cooking

Serves 6

Three-Bean Soup

Serves 6

TIP

Any combination of cooked beans will work well.

•

If cooking your own beans, use 1 cup (250 mL) of dry to make 3 cups (750 mL) cooked.

MAKE AHEAD

Prepare and refrigerate up to a day ahead and reheat gently before serving, adding more stock if too thick.

FROM
Rose Reisman's Enlightened Home Cooking

2 tsp	vegetable oil	10 mL
2 tsp	minced garlic	10 mL
3/4 cup	chopped onions	175 mL
3/4 cup	chopped carrots	175 mL
4 cups	chicken or vegetable stock	1 L
1 1/4 cups	canned chickpeas, drained	300 mL
1 1/4 cups	canned red kidney beans, drained	300 mL
1 1/4 cups	canned white kidney beans, drained	300 mL
1 tsp	dried basil	5 mL
1/4 cup	chopped fresh parsley	50 mL

1. In saucepan sprayed with vegetable spray, heat oil over medium heat; add garlic, onions and carrots and cook for 5 minutes or until onion is softened. Add chicken stock and 1 cup (250 mL) each of the chickpeas and red and white kidney beans; add basil. Bring to a boil. Cover, reduce heat to low and let simmer for 15 minutes or until carrots are tender.

2. Transfer soup to blender or food processor and purée. Return puréed soup to saucepan and stir in remaining 1/4 cup (50 mL) each chickpeas, red and white kidney beans. Cook gently for 5 minutes or until heated through. Serve garnished with parsley.

Serves 6

Vegetable and Bean Minestrone

1 tbsp	vegetable oil	15 mL
1 tsp	crushed garlic	5 mL
1 1/2 cups	finely chopped onions	375 mL
1	medium carrot, finely chopped	1
1	small celery stalk, finely chopped	1
4 1/2 cups	beef stock *or* chicken stock	1.125 L
1 1/2 cups	finely chopped peeled potatoes	375 mL
1 1/2 cups	chopped broccoli	375 mL
1	can (19 oz [540 mL]) tomatoes, crushed	1
3/4 cup	cooked chickpeas	175 mL
2	bay leaves	2
1 1/2 tsp	each dried basil and oregano	7 mL
1/3 cup	broken spaghetti	75 mL
1 tbsp	grated Parmesan cheese	15 mL

1. In large nonstick saucepan, heat oil; sauté garlic, onions, carrot and celery until softened, approximately 5 minutes.

2. Add stock, potatoes, broccoli, tomatoes, chickpeas, bay leaves, basil and oregano; cover and simmer for approximately 40 minutes or until vegetables are tender, stirring occasionally. Remove bay leaves. Season with pepper to taste.

3. Add pasta; cook for 10 minutes, stirring often, or until spaghetti is firm to the bite. Sprinkle with cheese.

TIP

Any vegetables or beans work well in this versatile soup.

If a main-dish soup is desired, add 8 oz (250 g) raw diced chicken or beef before simmering.

MAKE AHEAD

Make and refrigerate up to a day before and reheat gently before serving, adding more stock if too thick.

FROM
**Rose Reisman Brings Home
Light Cooking**

Roasted Tomato and Corn Soup

Serves 4 to 6

TIP

Regular fresh tomatoes can replace plum.

•

Dill or coriander can replace basil.

•

In the summer, grill tomatoes and 2 whole cobs of corn on barbecue.

MAKE AHEAD

Prepare soup up to 2 days in advance, adding more stock, if necessary, when reheating.

Freeze up to 4 weeks.

PREHEAT BROILER
TWO BAKING SHEETS LINED WITH ALUMINUM FOIL AND SPRAYED WITH VEGETABLE SPRAY

2 1/2 lbs	plum tomatoes (about 10)	1.25 kg
1	can (12 oz [341 mL]) corn, drained	1
2 tsp	vegetable oil	10 mL
2 tsp	minced garlic	10 mL
1 cup	chopped onions	250 mL
3/4 cup	finely chopped carrots	175 mL
2 1/2 cups	vegetable stock	625 mL
3 tbsp	tomato paste	45 mL
1/2 cup	chopped fresh basil (or 2 tsp [10 mL] dried)	125 mL

1. Put tomatoes on one baking sheet. With rack 6 inches (15 cm) under broiler, broil tomatoes about 30 minutes, turning occasionally, or until charred on all sides. Meanwhile, spread corn on other baking sheet and broil, stirring occasionally, about 15 minutes or until slightly browned. (Some corn kernels will pop.) When cool enough to handle, chop tomatoes.

2. In a nonstick saucepan, heat oil over medium–high heat. Add garlic, onions and carrots; cook 5 minutes or until softened and beginning to brown. Add roasted tomatoes, stock, tomato paste and, if using, dried basil. (If using fresh basil, wait until Step 3.) Bring to a boil; reduce heat to medium–low, cover and cook 20 minutes or until vegetables are tender.

FROM
Rose Reisman's Light Vegetarian Cooking

3. In food processor or blender, purée soup. Return to saucepan; stir in corn and, if using, fresh basil.

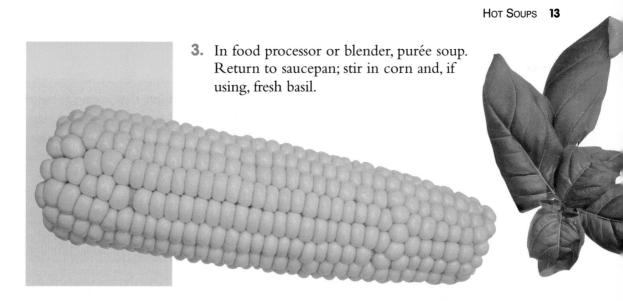

Serves 4 or 5

TIP

A small dollop of low-fat sour cream or yogurt followed by a sprinkling of the coriander gives this soup an elegant look.

Canned black beans can sometimes be difficult to find. Use 12 oz (375 g) cooked beans. One cup (250 mL) of dry beans yields approximately 3 cups (750 mL) cooked.

MAKE AHEAD

Prepare and refrigerate up to a day ahead and reheat gently before serving, adding more stock if too thick.

FROM
Rose Reisman's Enlightened Home Cooking

Black Bean Soup

2 tsp	vegetable oil	10 mL
2 tsp	minced garlic	10 mL
1 cup	chopped onions	250 mL
1 cup	chopped carrots	250 mL
1	can (19 oz [540mL]) black beans, drained (or 12 oz [375 g] cooked beans)	1
3 cups	chicken stock	750 mL
3/4 tsp	ground cumin	4 mL
1/4 cup	chopped coriander or parsley	50 mL

1. In a nonstick saucepan sprayed with vegetable spray, heat oil over medium heat; add garlic, onions and carrots and cook, stirring occasionally, for 4 minutes or until the onion is softened.

2. Add beans, stock and cumin; bring to a boil. Cover, reduce heat to medium low and simmer for 20 minutes or until carrots are softened. Transfer to food processor and purée until smooth.

3. Ladle into bowls; sprinkle with coriander.

Avocado Soup

Serves 2

Velvety and aromatic, this soup may be eaten hot or cold — although, if served cold, you'll need to make it the night before. In either case, the fried tortilla bits are essential, and must be added to the soup directly from the frying pan. Altogether, between the fried tortillas and oil-rich avocados, this is quite a calorific affair, so it should be followed by a light main course.

1	ripe avocado	1
1 tbsp	lime juice	15 mL
1	tomato	1
2 cups	vegetable stock	500 mL
2	green onions, minced	2
2 tbsp	vegetable oil	25 mL
2	small flour or corn tortillas, cut into small triangles	2
1/4 cup	finely diced cucumber	50 mL
	Few sprigs fresh coriander, roughly chopped	
	Optional: hot sauce or salsa	

1. Cut avocado in half, discard pit and spoon avocado flesh into bowl of food processor. Add lime juice.

2. Blanch tomato in boiling water for 30 seconds. Over a bowl, peel, core and deseed it. Chop tomato roughly and add to food processor. Strain any accumulated tomato juices from bowl and add to food processor.

3. In a saucepan, warm vegetable stock over low heat just until tepid. Add about half of it to food processor and blend at high speed for 30 seconds. Add the rest of the stock and blend for 1 minute more.

4. Transfer contents of food processor to a saucepan. Bring to a boil, stirring constantly, then lower heat to minimum and simmer, stirring frequently, for about 5 minutes. Add green onions; stir and simmer for 1 minute. Turn off heat, cover and let rest 5 to 10 minutes. (If serving cold, let soup cool down and refrigerate.)

5. In a sauté or frying pan, heat vegetable oil over high heat until it's just about to smoke. Add the tortillas and fry, turning over constantly, for 1 minute or until they are golden and crispy. Remove tortilla pieces and drain on a paper towel.

6. Ladle the soup into bowls. Garnish with tortilla triangles, cucumber and coriander. If desired, add a dollop of hot sauce or salsa in the middle. Serve immediately.

FROM
**The New Vegetarian Gourmet
by Byron Ayanoglu**

Red and Yellow Bell Pepper Soup

Serves 6

TIP

Orange peppers can be used instead of red or yellow.

•

If desired, coriander can be added before puréeing for a more intense flavor.

•

Roasted peppers in a jar (packed in water) can replace fresh peppers. Use about 4 oz (125 g) peppers in a jar for each fresh pepper required.

MAKE AHEAD

Roast peppers earlier in the day and set aside.

Prepare both soups earlier in day, and keep them separate until serving.

FROM
**Rose Reisman's Enlightened
Home Cooking**

PREHEAT OVEN TO BROIL

2	red bell peppers	2
2	yellow bell peppers	2
2 tsp	vegetable oil	10 mL
2 tsp	minced garlic	10 mL
1 1/2 cups	chopped onions	375 mL
1 1/4 cups	chopped carrots	300 mL
1/2 cup	chopped celery	125 mL
4 cups	chicken or vegetable stock	1 L
1 1/2 cups	diced, peeled potatoes	375 mL
	Pepper to taste	
1/4 cup	chopped fresh coriander, dill or basil	50 mL

1. Roast the peppers under the broiler for 15 to 20 minutes, turning several times until charred on all sides. Place in a bowl covered tightly with plastic wrap; let stand until cool enough to handle. Remove skin, stem and seeds.

2. In a nonstick saucepan sprayed with vegetable spray, heat oil over medium heat. Add garlic, onion, carrots and celery; cook for 8 minutes or until vegetables are softened, stirring occasionally. Add stock and potatoes; bring to a boil. Reduce heat to low; cover, and let cook for 20 to 25 minutes or until carrots and potatoes are tender.

3. Put the red peppers in food processor and process until smooth. Add half of the soup mixture to the red pepper purée and process until smooth. Season with pepper and pour into serving bowl. Rinse out food processor. Put yellow peppers in food processor and process until smooth; add remaining soup to yellow pepper purée and process until smooth. Season with pepper and pour into another serving bowl. To serve, ladle some of the red pepper soup into one side of individual bowl, at the same time ladling some of the yellow pepper soup into the other side of the bowl. Add coriander to soup and serve.

Serves 4

If you do not enjoy tarragon, omit it; the soup is delicious either way.

Used either canned, fresh or frozen corn niblets.

MAKE AHEAD

Prepare and refrigerate early in day and reheat gently before serving.

FROM
Rose Reisman Brings Home Light Cooking

Sweet Pea Soup

1 1/2 tsp	vegetable oil	7 mL
3/4 cup	chopped onion	175 mL
1 tsp	crushed garlic	5 mL
1	carrot, chopped	1
1/4 lb	mushrooms, sliced	125 g
3 cups	chicken stock	750 mL
1	medium potato, peeled and chopped	1
1	pkg (12 oz [350 g]) frozen sweet peas	1
1/2 cup	corn niblets	125 mL
2 tsp	dried tarragon (or 3 tbsp [45 mL] chopped fresh), optional	10 mL

1. In large nonstick saucepan, heat oil; sauté onion, garlic, carrot and mushrooms until softened, approximately 5 minutes.

2. Add stock, potato and all but 1/4 cup (50 mL) of the peas; reduce heat, cover and simmer for 20 to 25 minutes or until potato is tender.

3. Purée soup in food processor until creamy and smooth. Return to pan and add reserved peas and corn niblets. Season with tarragon (if using).

Serves 6 to 8

French Vegetable Soup

Despite the high profile of such French soups as onion and vichyssoise, the potage of choice in France (especially on countless table d'hôte menus) is a simple purée of vegetables. Here's a fail-safe version of this standard, with a couple of enhancements of my own. I cook the soup entirely free of butter or oil — which is just as well given the fat content of the croutons and garlic mayonnaise (Aïoli) that accompany it.

Be sure to wash leeks thoroughly, splitting down the middle and paying special care to the grit that hides where the green and white parts meet.

FROM
The New Vegetarian Gourmet
Byron Ayanoglu

PREHEAT OVEN TO 400° F (210° C)

1	small bunch of broccoli	1
8 cups	water	2 L
1 1/4 lbs	new potatoes, scrubbed	625 g
5 cups	leeks, green and white parts alike, roughly chopped	1.25 L
3	medium carrots, peeled	3
3	medium onions, roughly chopped	3
1 tsp	salt	5 mL
6 oz	green beans, trimmed and halved	150 g
2 cups	water	500 mL
4	thick slices of crusty bread, cut into 1-inch (2 cm) cubes	4
2 tbsp	olive oil	25 mL
1 tbsp	lemon juice	15 mL
1/2 cup	garlic mayonnaise	125 mL
	Few sprigs fresh parsley, chopped	

1. Trim broccoli, cutting off florets and chopping remaining stalk into 3 pieces. In a large saucepan or soup pot, bring water to a boil. Add broccoli stalk, potatoes, leeks, carrots, onions and salt. Return soup to boil; reduce heat to medium and cook without stirring for 20 to 25 minutes, until the potatoes and carrots are softened.

2. Add broccoli florets and green beans. Cook for 15 to 20 minutes, until vegetables are tender. Remove from heat and let cool.

3. In a food processor or blender, purée the soup in batches. Transfer the purée (it will be thick) back to the soup pot, and stir in the 2 cups (500 mL) of water to achieve desired consistency. Season to taste with salt and pepper.

4. Make the croutons: Spread bread cubes in a single layer on baking sheet. Drizzle olive oil evenly over cubes. Bake in oven for 8 to 10 minutes; turn croutons over and bake 5 minutes more, or until brown.

5. Reheat soup if necessary, stirring, until piping hot. Ladle the soup into wide soup plates. Sprinkle some lemon juice on each one, and garnish with the croutons. Drop a large dollop of garlic mayonnaise in the middle. Top with chopped parsley and serve immediately.

Curry-Fried Tofu Soup with Vegetables and Udon Noodles

FROM
New World Noodles
by Bill Jones and
Stephen Wong

Bouquet Garni

3	slices ginger root	3
1	garlic clove	1
1	stalk lemon grass, smashed and sliced *or* 1 tbsp (15 mL) lemon zest	1
2	star anise	2
2	thumb-sized pieces of dried tangerine peel, rinsed *or* 2 tsp (10 mL) orange zest	2

Soup

6 cups	vegetable stock *or* chicken stock	1.5 L
1	package (1 lb [500 g]) medium-firm tofu	1
2 tbsp	Madras curry powder	25 mL
1/4 tsp	salt	1 mL
4	packages (7 oz [200 g]) udon noodles *or* 1 lb (500 g) fresh spaghetti	4
2 cups	bean sprouts	500 mL
2 tbsp	vegetable oil	25 mL
1 cup	carrots, cut into matchsticks	250 mL
2 cups	broccoli florets	500 mL
1/2 tsp	salt	2 mL
4	sprigs cilantro	4

1. Wrap ingredients for *bouquet garni* in a piece of cheesecloth and tie securely with kitchen twine.

2. In a large saucepan or stockpot over high heat, bring bouquet garni and stock to a boil. Lower heat to medium and cook for 3 minutes. Cover and allow to steep for 15 minutes. Remove bouquet garni.

3. Cut tofu into 2-inch (5 cm) squares, about 1/2 inch (1 cm) thick. Pat dry with paper towels. In a mixing bowl, combine curry powder and salt; dredge tofu in mixture until lightly but evenly coated.

4. In a large pot of boiling salted water, cook noodles until *al dente*, about 2 minutes. Drain and divide between 4 bowls. Top with equally divided portions of bean sprouts.

5. In a nonstick wok or skillet, heat oil over medium–high heat for 30 seconds. Add tofu and fry until golden brown and slightly crisp on the outside, about 1 minute per side.

6. Meanwhile, bring broth to a boil. Add carrots and broccoli and cook until vegetables are just tender, about 3 minutes. Season with salt. Pour boiling broth and vegetables over noodle mixture. Top with tofu. Garnish with cilantro and serve immediately.

Serves 6

A good melting cheese with a nice nutty flavor (such as Gruyere or Raclette) works very well in this savory soup which warms you up on cold blustery days. The assertive flavor of onions mellows and sweetens when cooked until golden. This classic makes an easy transition from an everyday dish to an entertainment standout.

TIP

Buy French bread 3 to 4 inches (8 to 10 cm) in diameter. Or, if using a thin baguette, use 2 slices of bread in each bowl.

The onion soup base can be made ahead and refrigerated for up to 5 days or frozen for up to 3 months.

Hate shedding tears when chopping onions? To minimize the weeping problem, use a razor-sharp knife to prevent loss of juices and cover the cut onions with a paper towel as you chop them to prevent the vapors from rising to your eyes.

FROM
**The Comfort Food Cookbook
by Johanna Burkhard**

Cheese-Smothered Onion Soup

3 tbsp	butter	45 mL
8 cups	thinly sliced Spanish onions (about 2 to 3)	2 L
1/4 tsp	dried thyme	1 mL
1/4 tsp	pepper	1 mL
2 tbsp	all-purpose flour	25 mL
6 cups	beef stock	1.5 L
1 tbsp	olive oil	15 mL
1	large garlic clove, minced	1
6	slices French bread, about 3/4 inch (2 cm) thick	6
2 cups	shredded Gruyere cheese	500 mL

1. In a Dutch oven or large heavy saucepan, melt butter over medium heat. Add onions, thyme and pepper; cook, stirring often, for 15 minutes or until onions are tender and a rich golden color. Blend in flour; stir in stock. Bring to a boil, stirring until thickened. Reduce heat to medium-low, cover and simmer for 15 minutes.

2. Meanwhile, position oven rack 6 inches (15 cm) from broiler; preheat broiler.

3. In a small bowl, combine olive oil and garlic; lightly brush oil mixture over both sides of bread. Arrange on baking sheet; place under broiler and toast on both sides.

4. Place toasts in deep ovenproof soup bowls; sprinkle with half the cheese. Arrange bowls in large shallow baking pan. Ladle hot soup in bowls. Sprinkle with remaining cheese. Place under broiler for 3 minutes or until cheese melts and is lightly browned. Serve immediately.

Squash and Carrot Soup

TIP

For easier preparation, look for squash that has been pre-cut at your grocery store.

Onions can replace leeks.

Start with the smaller amount of stock, adding more if soup is too thick.

MAKE AHEAD

Prepare up to 2 days in advance. Reheat, adding extra stock if necessary.

Freeze up to 4 weeks.

FROM
Rose Reisman's Light Vegetarian Cooking

2 tsp	vegetable oil	10 mL
1 1/2 tsp	minced garlic	7 mL
1 1/2 cups	sliced leeks	375 mL
6 cups	chopped butternut squash (about 1 3/4 lbs [875 g])	1.5 L
3 1/2 to 4 1/2 cups	vegetable stock	875 mL to 1.125 L
1 cup	diced carrots	250 mL
1/2 tsp	dried thyme	2 mL
	Garnish (optional) 2% plain yogurt or light sour cream	

1. In a nonstick saucepan sprayed with vegetable spray, heat oil over medium-low heat. Stir in garlic and leeks; cook, covered, for 5 minutes or until softened.

2. Stir in squash, stock, carrots and thyme. Bring to a boil; reduce heat to medium-low, cover and cook 12 to 15 minutes or until vegetables are tender.

3. Transfer soup to a food processor or blender. Purée until smooth. Serve with a dollop of yogurt or sour cream, if desired.

Cabbage Beef Barley Soup

TIP

A squeeze of lemon juice and 2 tsp (10 mL) brown sugar give a sweet-and-sour quality to this soup.

•

The addition of beef bones enhances the intensity of this soup's flavor.

MAKE AHEAD

Prepare and refrigerate up to a day ahead and reheat gently before serving, adding more stock if too thick.

FROM
Rose Reisman's Enlightened Home Cooking

2 tsp	vegetable oil	10 mL
1 tsp	minced garlic	5 mL
1 cup	chopped onions	250 mL
1 cup	chopped carrots	250 mL
1/2 cup	chopped celery	125 mL
8 oz	boneless inside round steak, cut into 1/2-inch (1 cm) cubes	250 g
4 cups	shredded cabbage	1 L
1	can (19 oz [540 mL]) tomatoes, puréed	1
4 cups	beef stock *or* chicken stock	1 L
1 cup	peeled diced potatoes	250 mL
1/4 cup	barley	50 mL
1 1/2 tsp	caraway seeds	7 mL

1. In large nonstick saucepan sprayed with vegetable spray, heat oil over medium heat. Add garlic, onions, carrots, celery and steak; cook for 5 minutes or until beef is no longer pink. Add cabbage. Cook, stirring, for 2 minutes, or until cabbage wilts.

2. Add tomatoes, stock, potatoes, barley and caraway; bring to a boil. Cover, reduce heat to low and simmer for 35 to 40 minutes, or until barley is tender.

Aromatic Fish Soup

Fish soup is as much a part of life in the fish-rich Mediterranean as fishing itself. Every country has its own version, but the French claim the honor of the "state of the art," with their justly famous bouillabaisse. It is impossible for us to recreate any of the originals accurately, because we simply don't have the appropriate fish. But by using the right combination of aromatic vegetables, herbs and garlic — and by adding from our own available fish and seafood — we have come up with this delicious and utterly accessible version of a meal-size fish soup.

Fresh salmon heads are available cheaply at all fishmongers.

FROM
**Simply Mediterranean Cooking
by Byron Ayanoglu &
Algis Kemezys**

1/4 cup	olive oil	50 mL
1/2 tsp	salt	2 mL
1/2 tsp	freshly ground black pepper	2 mL
2 cups	roughly chopped onions	500 mL
4	stalks celery with leaves, cut into 1-inch (2.5 cm) pieces	4
1/2 tsp	fennel seeds	2 mL
2 lbs	plum tomatoes, diced *or* 1 can (28 oz [796 mL]) plum tomatoes	1 kg
10	cloves garlic, thinly sliced	10
2	bay leaves	2
1/2 tsp	dried basil	2 mL
1/2 tsp	dried oregano	2 mL
6 cups	water	1.5 L
	Few sprigs fresh parsley	
2 1/2 lbs	fish heads (about 2 salmon heads)	1.25 kg
2 cups	peeled cubed potatoes	500 mL
1 1/2 lbs	skinless boneless fillet of salmon, cod, halibut (or combination) cut into 1/2-inch (1 cm) cubes	750 g
8 oz	medium shrimp (optional), shelled and deveined	250 g
1 tbsp	lemon juice	15 mL
	Salt and pepper to taste	
4	large thick slices French bread, toasted	4
	Few chervil or celery leaves, chopped	

1. In a large saucepan over high heat, combine olive oil, salt and pepper. Add onions, celery and fennel seeds. Sauté, stirring frequently, for 5 minutes or until beginning to brown. Immediately add tomatoes, garlic, bay leaves, oregano and basil; cook, stirring, for 5 to 6 minutes or until sauce-like.

2. Stir in water; bring to boil. Add parsley and fish heads. Reduce heat to medium-high and cook for 35 to 40 minutes on a steady bubbling (but not rolling) boil, stirring infrequently.

3. Take off heat. Cover and let cool 1 to 2 hours to develop flavors. Strain, pushing down on ingredients and mashed down pulp to extract all the broth. Discard leftovers from strainer. (Recipe can be prepared to this point up to 2 days in advance;cover and refrigerate broth.)

4. Bring the strained broth to a boil. Add potatoes, reduce heat to medium-high and cook for 10 to 15 minutes or until soft and pierceable. Add fish and shrimp (if using); reduce heat to medium and cook 3 to 4 minutes or until the fish is tender but not overcooked. Stir in lemon juice. Season to taste with salt and pepper.

5. Place a toasted slice of bread into each of 4 bowls. Top each with one-quarter of the soup, making sure that potatoes and fish are distributed evenly. Garnish generously with chopped chervil and serve immediately.

Asparagus Ginger Sesame Cream Soup

Serves 4

This creamy, yet light, soup is bursting with the flavor of asparagus and ginger. In hot weather, it's excellent chilled.

For a special finish, garnish with asparagus cream. To make asparagus cream: Purée 4 spears of cooked asparagus in a food processor, then push through a strainer. Measure the purée and mix with an equal amount of sour cream. Place a spoonful of the mixture in the center of each serving and sprinkle with toasted sesame seeds.

1 tbsp	vegetable oil	15 mL
1	large onion, coarsely chopped	1
1 tbsp	minced ginger root	15 mL
8 oz	asparagus, trimmed and chopped	250 g
4 cups	chicken stock	1 L
1 cup	light (10%) cream	250 mL
1 tbsp	lemon juice	15 mL
1 tsp	sesame oil	5 mL
	Salt and pepper to taste	
2 tbsp	cornstarch dissolved in 4 tbsp (60 mL) water	25 mL
	Minced fresh herbs (chives, basil, rosemary, etc.), to taste	thyme,
1 tbsp	toasted sesame seeds	15 mL

1. In a large saucepan, heat oil over medium-high heat for 30 seconds. Add onion and ginger root; cook until the onion softens and begins to change color. Add asparagus and chicken stock; bring mixture to a boil. Reduce heat and simmer for 15 minutes or until the asparagus is cooked.

2. Remove saucepan from heat and allow to cool. Transfer mixture in batches to a blender or food processor and process until smooth.

3. Pour soup through a strainer, pushing as much purée through the mesh as possible (use the back of a wooden spoon to squeeze out liquid). Return liquid to saucepan, add cream and warm to a simmer. Add lemon juice, sesame oil; season with salt and pepper. Add dissolved cornstarch; bring soup to a boil, stirring constantly until thickened. Garnish with herbs, asparagus cream (directions appear at left), if desired, and toasted sesame seeds.

FROM
New World Chinese Cooking by Bill Jones and Stephen Wong

Serves 4 as a main course or 6 as a starter

This dish is a wonderful mixture of Indonesian spices and mussels in a complex tomato broth. Try cooking it in a Chinese sand hotpot and serve from the container along with a loaf of crusty sourdough bread.

FROM

New World Noodles by Bill Jones and Stephen Wong

Mussels in a Spiced Tomato Broth with Bean Thread Noodles

2 oz	bean thread noodles *or* angel hair pasta	50 g
1 tbsp	vegetable oil, plus oil for coating noodles	15 mL

Broth

1	onion, finely diced	1
1 tbsp	minced garlic	15 mL
1 tbsp	minced ginger root	15 mL
1 tsp	dried coriander seeds	5 mL
1 tsp	dried anise seeds	5 mL
1 tsp	mustard seeds	5 mL
1	cinnamon stick (or 1 tsp [5 mL] ground cinnamon)	1
1	stalk lemon grass, coarsely chopped *or* 1 tbsp (15 mL) lemon zest	1
4 cups	tomato juice	1L
2 cups	chicken or vegetable stock *or* clam juice	500 mL
	Hot pepper sauce to taste	
	Salt and pepper to taste	
2 lbs	fresh mussels	1 kg
	Chopped cilantro to taste	

1. In a heatproof bowl or pot, cover noodles with boiling water and soak for 3 minutes. Drain. (If using pasta, prepare according to package directions, drain and coat with a little oil.) Set aside.

2. In a large pot, heat oil over medium–high heat for 30 seconds. Add onion and cook until it softens and begins to change color. Add garlic and ginger root; sauté for 1 minute. Add coriander, anise and mustard seeds; toss while heating through to release flavors.

3. Add cinnamon, lemon grass, tomato juice and stock or clam juice; bring mixture to a boil. Reduce heat and simmer for 15 minutes. Season to taste with hot pepper sauce, salt and pepper. If possible, allow mixture to stand for 30 minutes to develop flavor. Strain broth through a fine mesh strainer and return to pot.

4. Bring broth back to a boil. Add mussels and noodles; cook until the mussels open. (Discard any that don't open.) Remove from heat and transfer to 4 warm bowls. Sprinkle with chopped cilantro and serve.

Clear Mushroom Soup

Serves 4

As delicious as it is digestible, this soup is perfect as the starter of a serious and/or festive meal. Low on fat, high on taste, it clears the palate and prepares the stomach for the onslaught to follow.

5 cups	Mushroom Stock (see recipe, opposite page)	1.25 L
3 tbsp	butter	45 mL
1/4 tsp	salt	1 mL
1/4 tsp	black pepper	1 mL
3 cups	sliced mushrooms (wild or regular)	750 mL
2 tbsp	lemon juice	25 mL
	Several sprigs fresh parsley	

1. In a saucepan, gradually warm mushroom stock over low heat until very hot. Do not boil.

2. Meanwhile, in a large frying pan melt butter over high heat for 1 minute until sizzling. Add salt and pepper and stir. Add sliced mushrooms and stir-fry for 5 to 6 minutes until browned. Remove from heat and stir in lemon juice.

3. Divide the mushrooms and pan juices among 4 soup bowls. Divide hot mushroom stock among bowls. Garnish with a decorative placing of 2 or 3 parsley leaves and serve immediately.

FROM
**The New Vegetarian Gourmet
Byron Ayanoglu**

Mushroom Stock

Serves 4

With its subtle mushroom flavor, this stock is the heart of a clean and tasty mushroom soup, as well as a creamless-but-creamy mushroom risotto that I adore.

This stock can also be used to great advantage in any sauce or other soups that would be enhanced by its delicate mushroom essence.

For sauces, prepare a concentrated version of this stock: Just boil down regular stock to reduce its volume by half.

FROM
**The New Vegetarian Gourmet
Byron Ayanoglu**

MAKES ABOUT 6 CUPS (1.5 L)

2 oz	dehydrated shiitake mushrooms	50 g
1/4 cup	olive oil	50 mL
Pinch	grated nutmeg	Pinch
1 1/2 cups	finely chopped celery leaves and/or stalks	375 mL
1 1/2 cups	finely chopped carrots	375 mL
1 1/2 cups	finely chopped onions	375 mL
8 cups	water	2 L
2	bay leaves	2
3	cloves	3
	Several sprigs fresh parsley and/or basil and/or coriander	
1 tsp	salt	5 mL

1. Place dehydrated shiitake mushrooms in a bowl and add sufficient boiling water to cover. Let mushrooms soak for 30 minutes, then drain (discarding liquid) and chop them into 1/2-inch (1 cm) pieces. Set aside.

2. In a large saucepan or soup pot, heat olive oil over medium-high heat for 1 minute. Add grated nutmeg and stir for 30 seconds. Add celery, carrots, onions and mushroom pieces. Cook, stirring often, for about 10 minutes, until volume of ingredients is reduced by about half.

3. Add water, stirring to deglaze the pot, and mix well. Add bay leaves, cloves and herb(s). Bring to boil, then reduce heat to low and let simmer undisturbed and uncovered for 30 to 35 minutes. Cover and let rest for 10 minutes.

4. Using a fine sieve, strain stock into a bowl. (Don't press down on solids; let gravity do the job.) Add salt to the stock. Store or use immediately.

Asparagus and Leek Soup

TIP

Choose the greenest asparagus with straight, firm stalks. The tips should be tightly closed and firm.

This soup can be served warm or cold.

MAKE AHEAD

Make and refrigerate up to a day before and reheat gently before serving, adding more stock if too thick.

FROM
**Rose Reisman Brings Home
Light Cooking**

3/4 lb	asparagus	375 g
1 1/2 tsp	vegetable oil	7 mL
1 tsp	crushed garlic	5 mL
1 cup	chopped onions	250 mL
2	leeks, sliced	2
3 1/2 cups	chicken stock	875 mL
1 cup	diced peeled potatoes	250 mL
	Salt and pepper	
2 tbsp	grated Parmesan cheese	25 mL

1. Trim asparagus; cut stalks into pieces and set tips aside.

2. In large nonstick saucepan, heat oil; sauté garlic, onions, leeks and asparagus stalks just until softened, approximately 10 minutes.

3. Add stock and potatoes; reduce heat, cover and simmer for 20 to 25 minutes or until vegetables are tender. Purée in food processor until smooth. Taste and adjust seasoning with salt and pepper. Return to saucepan.

4. Steam or microwave reserved asparagus tips just until tender; add to soup. Serve sprinkled with Parmesan cheese.

TIP

Try grilling or barbecuing corn on the cob until charred. Remove kernels with a knife.

Fresh basil as a garnish is excellent.

Great soup in just under 30 minutes.

MAKE AHEAD

Prepare up to 2 days in advance. Add more stock if necessary when reheating.

Freeze for up to 3 weeks.

Corn, Tomato and Zucchini Soup

2 tsp	vegetable oil	10 mL
1 tsp	minced garlic	5 mL
3 cups	diced zucchini	750 mL
1 1/2 cups	chopped onions	375 mL
3 cups	vegetable stock	750 mL
1	can (19 oz [540 mL]) whole tomatoes	1
1 1/4 cups	frozen or canned corn, drained	300 mL
2 tsp	dried basil	10 mL

1. In a nonstick saucepan sprayed with vegetable spray, heat oil over medium-high heat. Add garlic, zucchini and onions; cook for 5 minutes or until softened.

2. Stir in stock, tomatoes, corn, and basil. Bring to a boil, reduce heat to low and simmer 20 minutes, breaking up whole tomatoes with the back of a spoon.

FROM
Rose Reisman's Light Vegetarian Cooking

Cold Soups

Korean Cold Cucumber Soup

Serves 4

For a vegetarian version of this soup, replace fish sauce with a 2-inch (5 cm) square piece of dried kelp.

A few slices of apple or pear can be added to the soup; place them over the radish.

If you can find it, soak 1 tbsp (15 mL) dried wakame seaweed in several changes of cold water until tender. Drain and place in soup bowls under the cucumber slices.

Cucumber soup is really refreshing on a sultry summer day and helps to stimulate the appetite. This recipe is inspired by a cold Korean soup that combines cucumber and seaweed in a stock flavored with dried anchovies. I have removed the dried seaweed — it's relatively expensive and an acquired taste — and simplified the stock. If you're feeling adventurous, however, you can still put the seaweed back.

Toast sesame seeds in a dry pan over medium heat for 3 to 4 minutes until fragrant; remove from pan and allow to cool.

FROM
The Asian Bistro Cookbook by Andrew Chase

5 cups	water	1.25 L
5	slices ginger root	5
3	sprigs watercress	3
3	green onions, bottom two-thirds only, sliced *or* 1 small onion, sliced	3
1	small apple, sliced	1
4 tsp	fish sauce *or* 6 dried anchovies, heads removed	20 mL
1/2 tsp	black peppercorns	2 mL
2 tsp	rice vinegar *or* cider vinegar	10 mL
1 1/2 tsp	soya sauce	7 mL
1/4 tsp	granulated sugar	1 mL
1 1/2 cups	thinly sliced cucumbers	375 mL
1 tsp	salt	5 mL
2/3 cup	thinly sliced daikon radish *or* red or icicle radish	125 mL
2 tsp	salt	10 mL
1/4 tsp	sugar	1 mL
1 tsp	ground dried chilies (optional)	5 mL
1 1/2 tbsp	thinly sliced green onions	20 mL
1 tsp	toasted sesame seeds	5 mL

1. In a large saucepan, combine water, ginger, watercress, green onions, apple, fish sauce, and peppercorns. Bring to a boil; reduce heat and simmer 20 minutes. Add vinegar, soya sauce and sugar; cook 30 seconds. Strain stock into a large bowl; discard solids. Let stock cool to room temperature; refrigerate.

2. In a bowl, combine cucumbers and 1 tsp (5 mL) salt. In another bowl, combine radish and 2 tsp (10 mL) salt. Set bowls aside for 30 minutes. In a sieve, quickly rinse cucumber under cold running water; drain, squeezing solids hard to remove extra moisture. Refrigerate. Repeat draining procedure with radish; transfer to a bowl and stir in sugar and, if using, chilies. Refrigerate at least 1 hour. Soak green onions rings in cold water.

3. Mound the cucumber slices in 4 individual soup bowls and top with radish. Carefully ladle stock into bowls without disturbing mounded vegetables; sprinkle with drained green onion rings and toasted sesame seeds.

Dill Carrot Soup

Serves 4 to 6

TIP

This soup can be served hot or cold.

A dollop of yogurt on each bowlful enhances both the appearance and flavor.

MAKE AHEAD

Make and refrigerate up to a day before. If serving warm, reheat gently.

FROM
Rose Reisman Brings Home Light Cooking

1 lb	carrots, sliced (6 to 8 medium)	500 g
2 tsp	vegetable oil	10 mL
2 tsp	crushed garlic	10 mL
1 cup	chopped onions	250 mL
3 1/2 cups	chicken stock	875 mL
3/4 cup	2% milk	175 mL
2 tbsp	chopped fresh dill (or 1 tsp [5 mL] dried dillweed)	25 mL
2 tbsp	chopped fresh chives *or* green onions	25 mL

1. In large saucepan of boiling water, cook carrots just until tender. Drain and return to saucepan; set aside.

2. In nonstick skillet, heat oil; sauté garlic and onions until softened, approximately 5 minutes. Add to carrots along with stock; cover and simmer for 25 minutes.

3. Purée in food processor until smooth, in batches if necessary. Return to saucepan; stir in milk, dill and chives.

Asian Gazpacho

Serves 4 to 6

When tomatoes are ripe and plentiful and the weather is still warm, a cold tomato-based soup is wonderfully refreshing. But few Asian countries, apart from Korea and Japan, have a tradition of making cold soups. The Chinese make cold, sweet soups, but only for dessert. In the Filipino capital city of Manila, however, they still serve traditional gazpacho — a legacy of Spanish colonialism. While Spanish gazpacho is as much a cucumber soup as it is a tomato soup, this version definitely places the emphasis on tomatoes.

FROM
**The Asian Bistro Cookbook
by Andrew Chase**

2	green finger chilies, seeded and finely chopped	2
1/4 cup	peanut oil *or* vegetable oil	50 mL
2	green onions, cut into short lengths	2
2 or 3	cloves garlic, smashed lightly with the side of a knife	2 or 3
1/4 cup	finely chopped red or sweet white onions	50 mL
3 lbs	ripe tomatoes	1.5 kg
2 tbsp	grated ginger root	25 mL
1 tbsp	fish sauce *or* light soya sauce	15 mL
1 cup	finely chopped, peeled, seeded cucumber	250 mL
1/2 cup	finely chopped bell peppers (optional)	125 mL
1/4 cup	roughly chopped mint and/or coriander leaves	50 mL
2 tbsp	lime juice	25 mL
	Salt to taste	
6	dried red chilies	6
	Lime wedges and mint and/or coriander leaves for garnish	

1. Place chilies in a bowl. In a small saucepan, heat oil over medium heat; green onions cook until they start to brown. Add garlic; cook until golden. Pour through a strainer over chilies; set chili oil aside to cool. Remove green onion from strainer and discard. Finely chop garlic cloves and set aside.

2. In a large bowl, add cold water to cover onions; let stand 20 minutes. Drain and set aside.

3. In a large pot of boiling water, blanch tomatoes 20 seconds; drain. Rinse under cold running water. Over a bowl, peel, core and seed them; finely chop tomato flesh and add to onions. Strain accumulated juices from bowl; add to tomatoes and onions.

continued on page 42

4. In a small bowl, stir together ginger, fish sauce and 2 tbsp (25 mL) water. Strain through a piece of cheese-cloth over tomato-onion mixture, squeezing to extract juice. Stir in cucumber, peppers (if using), mint or coriander, lime juice and chili oil until well mixed. Season to taste with salt. Thin with water or tomato juice to desired consistency. Chill 30 minutes or until cool.

5. In dry frying pan over medium heat, toast dried chilies until darkened but not black. Transfer chilies to a spice grinder (or mortar and pestle) and grind to a reasonably fine powder. Garnish chilled gazpacho with lime wedges and herb leaves. Serve with roasted chili powder for seasoning to taste.

FROM
**The New Vegetarian Gourmet
Byron Ayanoglu**

Cold Mango Soup

2 tsp	vegetable oil	10 mL
1/2 cup	chopped onions	125 mL
2 tsp	minced garlic	10 mL
2 cups	vegetable stock	500 mL
2 1/2 cups	chopped ripe mango (about 2 large)	625 mL
	Garnish (optional)	
	2% plain yogurt	
	Coriander leaves	

1. In a nonstick saucepan, heat oil over medium heat. Add onions and garlic; cook, stirring, 4 minutes or until browned.

2. Add stock. Bring to a boil; reduce heat to medium-low and cook 5 minutes or until onions are soft.

3. Transfer mixture to a food processor. Add 2 cups (500 mL) of the mango. Purée until smooth. Stir in remaining chopped mango.

4. Chill 2 hours or until cold. Serve with a dollop of yogurt and garnish with coriander, if desired.

Cold Two-Melon Soup

Serves 4

TIP

This is a terrific summer soup.

Adjust sugar to taste.

MAKE AHEAD

Prepare early in day and chill.

FROM
Rose Reisman's Light Vegetarian Cooking

6 cups	cubed ripe honeydew or other green melon	1.5 L
2 tsp	grated lime zest	10 mL
1/4 cup	freshly squeezed lime juice	50 mL
1/4 cup	granulated sugar	50 mL
3 cups	cubed ripe cantaloupe	750 mL
1 tbsp	orange juice concentrate	15 mL
1 tsp	grated orange zest	5 mL
	Mint sprigs	

1. In a food processor, purée honeydew melon, lime zest, lime juice, and 2 tbsp (25 mL) of the sugar until smooth. Transfer to a bowl.

2. Rinse out bowl of food processor. Add cantaloupe, orange juice concentrate, orange zest and remaining sugar; purée until smooth. Transfer to a separate bowl.

3. Chill both soups 30 minutes or until cold.

4. To serve, ladle 1 cup (250 mL) green soup into each of 4 individual serving bowls. Carefully pour 1/2 cup (125 mL) orange soup into the center. Garnish with mint sprigs and serve.

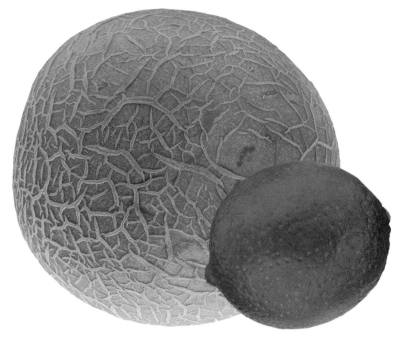

Meat Stews

Serves 4

During the long winter months, this is the kind of hearty, legume-based stew with which southern europeans bring the sunshine back into their homes. The version we present here is virtually foolproof, requiring just a minimum of attention — and little effort if one uses canned chickpeas (washed with cold running water and strained). Leftovers are wonderful, since the flavors will intensify upon reheating the next day. It can be enjoyed as a vegetarian main course (just omit the sausages) or you can experiment with substitutes for the sausage; any stewing meat (pork, lamb or chicken) will work well. In all cases, the stew is wonderful if served with a salad and crusty bread.

FROM
**Simply Mediterranean Cooking
by Byron Ayanoglu & Algis
Kemezys**

Potato and Chickpea Stew with Spicy Sausage

1/2 cup	red lentils *(masoor dal)*	125 mL
1 cup	diced peeled potatoes	250 mL
1/2 cup	scraped carrots, cut into 1/4-inch (5 mm) cubes	125 mL
	Boiling water	
1/4 cup	olive oil	50 mL
1 tsp	sweet paprika	5 mL
3/4 tsp	salt	4 mL
1/4 tsp	freshly ground black pepper	1 mL
1/4 tsp	turmeric	1 mL
2 cups	chopped onions	500 mL
1/4 tsp	chili flakes	1 mL
2 tbsp	finely chopped garlic	25 mL
2	medium tomatoes, cut into 1/2-inch (1 cm) wedges	2
2	bay leaves	2
1 tsp	red wine vinegar	5 mL
1/2 tsp	dried oregano	2 mL
1/2 tsp	dried thyme	2 mL
2 cups	cooked chickpeas *or* 1 can (19 oz [540 mL]) chickpeas, rinsed and drained	500 mL
2	dried figs, cut into 1/4-inch (5 mm) cubes	2
1 lb	spicy sausage (such as merguez, chorizo or spicy Italian)	500 g
2 tbsp	finely minced red onions	25 mL
	Few sprigs fresh parsley, chopped	

1. Soak lentils in boiling water to cover for 20 minutes; drain. Bring 5 cups (1.25 L) water to a boil; stir in lentils and cook 5 minutes. Add potatoes and carrots; return to a boil. Reduce heat to medium; cook, stirring very occasionally, for 10 minutes or until the potatoes are tender, but not quite crumbling. Drain, reserving cooking liquid. Set lentils and vegetables aside. Measure out 1 1/2 cups (375 mL) of the cooking liquid and set aside. (If there isn't enough liquid, make up the difference with water.)

continued on page 48

2. In a large deep saucepan, heat olive oil over medium-high heat. Add paprika, salt, pepper and turmeric; cook, stirring, for 1 minute, being careful not to let the spices burn. Add onions and chili flakes; cook, stirring, 4 minutes until the onions are soft and beginning to catch on the bottom of the pan. Add garlic and cook, stirring, for 1 minute. Add tomatoes, bay leaves, vinegar, oregano and thyme; cook, stirring, for 2 to 3 minutes or until tomatoes are starting to break up and a sauce forms.

3. Stir in lentil-vegetable mixture, chickpeas, figs and reserved cooking liquid; bring to a boil. Reduce heat to medium-low and cook for 20 minutes, uncovered, stirring occasionally from the bottom up to avoid scorching. Take off heat, cover and let rest for 10 minutes.

4. While stew rests, grill, broil or fry the sausages. Serve stew garnished with sausages, red onions and parsley.

Chicken Fagioli
(Bean Tomato Sauce)

TIP

Use bone-in chicken breasts instead of legs; reduce browning time to 4 minutes and reduce cooking time to 20 minutes.

White kidney beans or a combination can be used.

A great dish to reheat.

MAKE AHEAD

Brown chicken earlier in the day and refrigerate until ready to cook with sauce.

4	chicken legs	4
1/4 cup	all-purpose flour	50 mL
2 tsp	vegetable oil	10 mL
2 tsp	minced garlic	10 mL
1/2 cup	chopped onions	125 mL
1/3 cup	chopped carrots	75 mL
1/3 cup	chopped celery	75 mL
1 1/2 cups	red kidney beans, drained	375 mL
1 cup	puréed canned tomatoes	250 mL
3/4 cup	chicken stock	175 mL
1 1/2 tsp	dried basil	7 mL
1 tsp	dried oregano	5 mL

1. In large nonstick skillet sprayed with vegetable spray, heat 1 tsp (5 mL) of the oil over high heat. Dust chicken with flour and cook for 8 minutes, turning often, or until browned on all sides. Set aside and wipe skillet clean.

2. Reduce heat to medium. Add remaining 1 tsp (5 mL) oil to skillet. Add garlic, onions, carrots and celery; cook for 5 minutes or until softened. Mash 1/2 cup (125 mL) of the kidney beans; add mashed and whole beans, tomatoes, stock, basil and oregano to skillet. Bring to a boil, reduce heat to medium-low, add browned chicken pieces, cover and cook for 30 minutes or until juices run clear when legs are pierced at thickest point. Stir occasionally. Remove skin before eating.

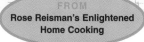

FROM
Rose Reisman's Enlightened Home Cooking

Every cook has a special version of chili. Here's mine — it's meaty and nicely spiced with just the right amount of beans. Not everyone agrees that beans belong in a chili — witness the Texas version dubbed "bowl of red" — but I love the way the beans absorb the spices and rich tomato flavor.

TIP

The flavor of the chili hinges on the quality of chili powder used. Most powders are a blend of dried, ground mild chilies, as well as cumin, oregano, garlic and salt. Read the list of ingredients to be sure you're not buying one with starch and sugar fillers. Chili powder should not be confused with powdered or ground chilies of the cayenne pepper variety.

Amazing Chili

1 1/2 lbs	lean ground beef	750 g
2	medium onions, chopped	2
3	cloves garlic, finely chopped	3
2	stalks celery, chopped	2
1	large sweet green pepper, chopped	1
2 tbsp	chili powder	25 mL
1 1/2 tsp	dried oregano	7 mL
1 1/2 tsp	ground cumin	7 mL
1 tsp	salt	5 mL
1/2 tsp	red pepper flakes, or to taste	2 mL
1	can (28 oz [796 mL]) tomatoes, chopped, juice reserved	1
1 cup	beef stock	250 mL
1	can (19 oz [540 mL]) pinto or red kidney beans, drained and rinsed	1
1/4 cup	chopped fresh parsley or coriander	50 mL

1. In a Dutch oven, brown beef over medium-high heat, breaking up with back of a spoon, for about 7 minutes or until no longer pink.

2. Reduce heat to medium. Add onions, garlic, celery, green pepper, chili powder, oregano, cumin, salt and red pepper flakes; cook, stirring often, for 5 minutes or until vegetables are softened.

3. Stir in the tomatoes with juice and the stock. Bring to a boil; reduce heat, cover and simmer, stirring occasionally, for 1 hour.

4. Add beans and parsley; cover and simmer for 10 minutes more.

Chicken Breast Caponata

Serves 3 or 4

Eggplant is a magical vegetable that starts out dry and porous as a sponge, then cooks up oily-smooth and sweet, enhancing everything that is served with it, including chicken. Here we combine chicken and eggplant with the usual ingredients of caponata (minus the garlic) for a gently perky concoction that pleases the palate without jarring it.

FROM
Simply Mediterranean Cooking by Byron Ayanoglu & Algis Kemezys

2 cups	peeled eggplant, cut into 1/2-inch (1 cm) cubes	500 mL
3 tbsp	olive oil	45 mL
1/4 tsp	freshly ground black pepper	1 mL
1	medium onion, sliced	1
8 oz	skinless boneless chicken breast, cut into 1/2-inch (1 cm) strips	250 g
2 cups	plum tomatoes, peeled and cut into 1/2-inch (1 cm) cubes or canned tomatoes	500 mL
1 tbsp	drained capers	15 mL
1 tsp	dried basil	5 mL
1 tbsp	balsamic vinegar	15 mL
1/4 tsp	salt	1 mL
8	black olives, pitted and halved	8
	Steamed rice as an accompaniment	
	Few sprigs fresh basil or parsley, chopped	
	Grated Romano cheese	

1. Bring a pot of salted water to the boil while peeling and cutting eggplant. (Keep in mind that eggplant doesn't like to wait long after it's cut and will quickly turn brown.) Add eggplant to the boiling water, reduce heat to medium and cook 5 to 6 minutes or until eggplant is tender and softened. Drain and set aside.

2. In a large nonstick frying pan, heat oil and pepper over high heat for 1 minute. Add onion and stir-fry for 1 minute. Add chicken and stir-fry for 30 seconds. Add eggplant; stir-fry 2 to 3 minutes or until the chicken firms up and everything else is shiny and starting to brown.

3. Immediately add tomatoes, capers, basil, vinegar and salt; cook, stirring, for 4 minutes or until tomatoes are breaking up and a thick sauce has formed. Reduce heat to medium, scatter olives, cover and cook for just 1 minute. Take off heat. Let rest, covered, for 5 minutes.

4. Arrange on plates with steamed rice, garnish with chopped fresh basil and a dusting of grated cheese. Serve immediately.

Serves 4

Couscous with Raisins, Dates and Curry

TIP

This dish is fine served at room temperature.

•

Try adding 1/4 cup (50 mL) diced carrots to vegetables.

MAKE AHEAD

Prepare up to the day before, then gently reheat over low heat.

1 1/4 cups	chicken stock	300 mL
3/4 cup	couscous	175 mL
1 tbsp	margarine	15 mL
3/4 cup	finely chopped onions	175 mL
1 tsp	crushed garlic	5 mL
1 cup	finely chopped red bell peppers	250 mL
1/4 cup	raisins	50 mL
1 tsp	curry powder	5 mL
5	dried dates or apricots, chopped	5

1. In small saucepan, bring chicken stock to boil. Stir in couscous and remove from heat. Cover and let stand until liquid is absorbed, 5 to 8 minutes. Place in serving bowl.

2. Meanwhile, in nonstick saucepan, melt margarine; sauté onions, garlic and red peppers until softened, approximately 5 minutes. Add raisins, curry powder and dates; mix until combined. Add to couscous and mix well.

FROM
Rose Reisman Brings Home Light Cooking

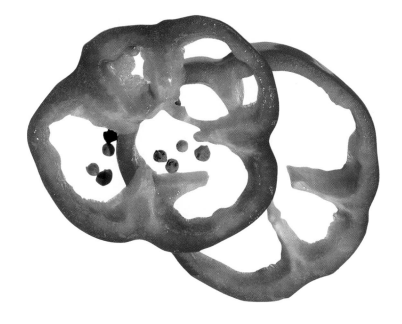

Serves 4 to 6

Turkey Ratatouille Chili

TIP

Great combination of ratatouille and chili in one dish.

Great as a family meal. Serve with french bread.

Ground pork, veal or chicken can replace turkey.

MAKE AHEAD

Prepare up to a day ahead and reheat gently, adding extra chicken stock if too thick.

2 tsp	vegetable oil	10 mL
2 tsp	minced garlic	10 mL
1 cup	chopped onions	250 mL
1 2/3 cups	chopped zucchini	400 mL
1 2/3 cups	chopped peeled eggplant	400 mL
1 1/2 cups	chopped mushrooms	375 mL
12 oz	ground turkey	375 g
2 tbsp	tomato paste	25 mL
1	can (19 oz [540 mL]) tomatoes, puréed	1
2 cups	chicken stock	500 mL
1 1/3 cups	peeled chopped potatoes	325 mL
1 cup	canned red kidney beans, drained	250 mL
1 tbsp	chili powder	15 mL
1 1/2 tsp	dried basil	7 mL
1	bay leaf	1

1. In large nonstick saucepan sprayed with vegetable spray, heat oil over medium heat. Add garlic, onions, zucchini and eggplant; cook for 5 minutes or until softened. Add mushrooms and cook 2 minutes longer. Remove vegetables from skillet and set aside. Add turkey to skillet and cook for 3 minutes, stirring to break it up, or until no longer pink. Drain fat and add cooked vegetables to skillet.

2. Add tomato paste, tomatoes, stock, potatoes, beans, chili powder, basil and bay leaf; bring to a boil. Cover, reduce heat to low and simmer for 40 minutes, stirring occasionally.

FROM
Rose Reisman's Enlightened Home Cooking

Stewed Beef with Whole Garlic, Hoisin and Barley

Serves 4 to 6

This hearty dish is a great cool-weather warmer.

Refrigerating overnight actually helps to develop the flavor of this stew. Reheat on top of the stove, over medium-low heat, stirring occasionally to prevent the stew from sticking and thin with additional stock or water, if required.

4 tbsp	all-purpose flour	60 mL
	Salt and pepper to taste	
1 lb	stewing beef, cut into 1-inch (2.5 cm) cubes	500 g
1 tbsp	vegetable oil	15 mL
1	medium onion, cut into 1/2-inch (1 cm) dice	1
1	head garlic, cloves peeled	1
2	medium carrots, cut into 1-inch (2.5 cm) dice	2
1 cup	pearl barley	250 mL
6 cups	beef stock	1.5 L
3 tbsp	hoisin sauce	45 mL
1 tbsp	dark soya sauce	15 mL
1 tsp	chili sauce	5 mL
1 tbsp	chopped cilantro	15 mL
	Salt and pepper to taste	

1. In a plastic bag, combine flour, salt and pepper. Add beef and shake until thoroughly coated.

2. In a large pot, heat oil over high heat for 30 seconds. Add dredged beef and stir-fry until the meat begins to brown, about 5 minutes. Add onion, garlic, carrots and barley; cook for 3 minutes. Add beef stock, hoisin sauce, soya sauce, chili sauce and cilantro; bring to a boil. Reduce heat and simmer 40 minutes or until beef is tender and the barley is soft. Season with salt and pepper. Serve over steamed rice or mashed potatoes.

FROM
**New World Chinese Cooking
by Bill Jones and
Stephen Wong**

What's more comforting than a satisfying stew? You start feeling good the minute you set this one-pot dish to simmer on the stovetop. As the herb-infused aroma wafts through your kitchen the good feeling grows. The first forkful confirms that this stew is comfort food at its best. What's more, it can comfort you all over again the next day with easy-to-reheat leftovers. Delicious served with crusty bread to mop up the flavorful sauce.

TIP

To give your stew a rich, dark color, leave meat out of the refrigerator for 20 minutes; blot with paper towels before browning. Cook beef in small batches for best browning and reheat pan before adding each new batch of meat. I find fresh meat browns better than frozen meat that has been defrosted.

FROM
The Comfort Food Cookbook by Johanna Burkhard

Old-Fashioned Beef Stew

1/4 cup	all-purpose flour	50 mL
1 tsp	salt	5 mL
1/2 tsp	pepper	2 mL
2 tbsp	vegetable oil (approximate)	25 mL
1 1/2 lbs	stewing beef, cut into cubes 1 1/2 inches (4 cm) square	750 g
2	medium onions, chopped	2
3	cloves garlic, finely chopped	3
1 tsp	dried thyme	5 mL
1 tsp	dried marjoram	5 mL
1	bay leaf	1
1 cup	red wine *or* additional beef stock	250 mL
3 tbsp	tomato paste	45 mL
3 cups	beef stock (approximate)	750 mL
5	carrots	5
2	stalks celery	2
1 1/2 lbs	potatoes (about 5)	750 g
12 oz	green beans	375 g
1/4 cup	chopped fresh parsley	50 mL

1. Combine flour, salt and pepper in a heavy plastic bag. In batches, add beef to flour mixture and toss to coat. Transfer to a plate. Reserve remaining flour mixture.

2. In a Dutch oven, heat half the oil over medium–high heat; cook beef in batches, adding more oil as needed, until browned all over. Transfer to a plate.

3. Reduce heat to medium–low. Add onions, garlic, thyme, marjoram, bay leaf and remaining flour to pan; cook, stirring, for 4 minutes or until softened. Add wine and tomato paste; cook, stirring, to scrape up brown bits. Return beef and any accumulated juices to pan; pour in stock.

4. Bring to a boil, stirring, until slightly thickened. Reduce heat, cover and simmer over medium–low heat, stirring occasionally, for 1 hour.

5. Meanwhile, peel carrots and halve lengthwise. Cut carrots and celery into 1 1/2-inch (4 cm) chunks. Peel potatoes and quarter. Add vegetables to pan. Cover and simmer for 30 minutes.

continued on page 58

6. Trim ends of beans and cut into 2-inch (5 cm) lengths. Stir into stew mixture, adding more stock if necessary, until vegetables are just covered. Cover and simmer for 30 minutes more or until vegetables are tender. Remove bay leaf and stir in parsley. Adjust seasoning with salt and pepper to taste.

Filipino Turmeric-Scented Pork Stew

For a slightly different flavor, first brown shallots or pearl onions in 1 1/2 tsp (7 mL) oil; remove from pan and lightly brown pork pieces, then add garlic and dry spices; cook 30 seconds, add other ingredients and return shallots or onions to the pan and proceed as above.

•

Fresh turmeric root is often available at Southeast Asian or Indian grocers. It has a very raw taste and is best dry-roasted before using. To use here, first toast 1 1/4 tsp (6 mL) very thin slices of turmeric in a dry pan over medium heat until color darkens and the slices become fairly dry; it should be extremely fragrant by then. Either first pound into a powder or add slices directly to the stew. Another simple home-style dish from the northern part of the Philippines, this vinegar-based stew has an unusual, delicate flavor and a pleasing color. It's a cinch to put together and cook. The only somewhat unusual ingredient, chayote squash, is often available at regular supermarkets and always available at Asian, Caribbean and South American grocers. It can be replaced with another green-fleshed squash, such as vegetable marrow or zucchini, or green papaya, but these will not provide the same uniquely light taste and texture. Serve with rice.

FROM
The Asian Bistro Cookbook by Andrew Chase

1 1/2 lbs	pork, butt or shoulder, cut into 1 1/2-inch (4 cm) cubes	750 g
1 tsp	minced ginger root	5 mL
1 tbsp	minced garlic	15 mL
3	bay leaves	3
6	cloves or 1/4 tsp (1 mL) ground cloves	6
2	2-inch (5 cm) pieces Asian cinnamon stick or cinnamon stick	2
1 tsp	ground turmeric	5 mL
1/8 tsp	black pepper	0.5 mL
1/4 cup	rice vinegar	50 mL
3 tbsp	fish sauce *or* 6 finely chopped anchovies mixed in 2 tbsp (25 mL) water	45 mL
1/2 cup	small whole shallots or pearl onions (optional)	125 mL
1 to 1 1/2 cups	peeled, cored and cubed chayote squash or green papaya or another green-fleshed squash	250 to 375 mL
1 cup	green peas, fresh or frozen	250 mL
1 3/4 tsp	cornstarch dissolved in 2 tsp (10 mL) water	9 mL
1 tbsp	finely chopped Chinese celery or regular celery	15 mL
1 tsp	finely chopped mint or parsley (optional)	5 mL

1. In a saucepan combine pork, vinegar, fish sauce, garlic, ginger, turmeric, pepper, cloves, bay leaves, cinnamon and shallots, if using; mix well. Let stand 10 to 15 minutes.

2. Bring to a boil, reduce heat to simmer; cover and cook 45 minutes or until meat is tender. Stir in squash and fresh peas, if using; cook, covered, 10 minutes or until squash is tender. Stir in frozen peas, if using; cook 1 minute longer. Bring to a boil and stir in cornstarch mixture; reduce heat to simmer and cook 1 minute. Stir in celery; cook 20 seconds. Serve garnished with mint or parsley, if desired.

Cassoulet with Pork and Zucchini

Serves 6

Baked beans take many forms around the world, and cassoulet is the version favored in the well-fed northern regions of France. There, any number of fatty meats (goose and/or pork fat, for example) are mixed with beans and baked under an equally fatty crust. Here we "Mediterraneanize" the original recipe, using additional vegetables and a lot less fat. Still, this is a hefty and lengthy dish that requires cool weather, a suitable occasion (to justify the effort), and a well- ventilated room.

FROM
**Simply Mediterranean Cooking
by Byron Ayanoglu & Algis
Kemezys**

DEEP BAKING DISH, MEASURING ABOUT 12 BY 16 INCHES (30 BY 40 CM)

1 tbsp	olive oil	15 mL
1/4 tsp	salt	1 mL
1/4 tsp	freshly ground black pepper	1 mL
1 lb	pork tenderloin, cut into 1-inch (2.5 cm) cubes	500 g
1 tbsp	finely chopped garlic	15 mL
1 tbsp	olive oil	15 mL
1/2 tsp	salt	2 mL
1/2 tsp	freshly ground black pepper	2 mL
1 cup	finely diced onions	250 mL
2	medium leeks, trimmed, washed and finely chopped (about 3 cups [750 mL])	2
2	stalks celery with leaves, finely chopped	2
Half	green pepper, finely diced	Half
1	large carrot, scraped and finely diced (about 4 oz [125 g])	1
8 oz	mushrooms, trimmed and quartered	250 g
1 lb	tomatoes, peeled and finely chopped (about 2 cups [500 mL]) *or* canned tomatoes	500 g
1 tbsp	tomato paste, diluted in 1 cup (250 mL) water	15 mL
1 tsp	red wine vinegar	5 mL
1 tsp	dried basil	5 mL
1 tsp	dried oregano	5 mL
2 cups	cooked white kidney beans *or* 1 can (19 oz [540 mL]), rinsed and drained	500 mL
2 cups	cooked red Romano beans *or* 1 can (19 oz [540 mL]), rinsed and drained	500 mL
1	medium zucchini cut into 1/4-inch (5 mm) rounds (about 8 oz [250 g])	1
2 cups	chicken stock	500 mL

Topping

2 cups	breadcrumbs	500 mL
1 tbsp	finely chopped garlic	15 mL
1/2 tsp	ground allspice	2 mL
2	eggs, beaten	2
2 tbsp	olive oil	25 mL
1 cup	dry white vermouth or white wine	250 mL
	Few sprigs fresh parsley, chopped	

1. In a large nonstick frying pan, heat 1 tbsp (15 mL) olive oil, salt and pepper over high heat for 30 seconds. Add pork and stir-fry for 2 minutes, turning meat often so that all the pieces are thoroughly browned. Add garlic and stir-fry 1 more minute. Transfer contents of the frying pan to a large saucepan.

2. Return the frying pan to high heat. Add 1 tbsp (15 mL) olive oil, salt and pepper; heat for 30 seconds. Add onions, leeks, celery, green pepper, carrot and mushrooms; cook, stirring, for 4 minutes or until the vegetables are softened and a little oily. Transfer vegetables to saucepan with meat.

3. Stir in tomatoes, diluted tomato paste, vinegar, dried basil and oregano. Bring to a boil, cover tightly, reduce heat to medium–low and cook for 25 to 30 minutes or until the meat is cooked through. Remove from heat.

4. Preheat oven to 375° F (190° C). Add white kidney beans, red Romano beans, zucchini and chicken stock to the stew. Gently fold to mix everything thoroughly. Transfer this mixture to baking dish. Spread mixture over bottom of dish, making a layer about 1 1/2-inches (4 cm) deep.

5. Make the topping: In a bowl, stir together the bread-crumbs, garlic and allspice until combined. In a small bowl, combine the eggs, olive oil and vermouth. Add this liquid to the breadcrumbs and stir to mix until combined (it'll be wet and lumpy).

6. As evenly as possible, spread this topping over the stew. Bake uncovered for 30 minutes. Remove from oven and press the topping (which will have browned a little) just into the stew, but leaving it still on top. Put back in the oven and bake another 30 minutes until the topping is nicely crusted and the stew is bubbling underneath.

7. Remove from oven and let rest 10 minutes. Portion onto plates, keeping breadcrumbs on top; garnish with chopped parsley and serve immediately.

TIP

Substitute stewing beef or veal for leg of lamb.

•

Vegetables of your own choice can replace those in recipe.

•

Do not use a food processor to purée potatoes as they will become sticky.

•

Great as leftovers.

MAKE AHEAD

Prepare mashed potatoes recipe up to a day ahead. Reheat gently before serving.

Prepare stew early in the day and gently reheat before serving.

Lamb Vegetable Stew over Garlic Mashed Potatoes

3 tsp	vegetable oil	15 mL
12 oz	leg of lamb, visible fat removed, cut into 1-inch (2.5 cm) cubes	375 g
3 tbsp	flour	45 mL
1 cup	pearl onions	250 mL
2 tsp	minced garlic	10 mL
1 1/2 cups	sliced mushrooms	375 mL
1 1/2 cups	chopped leeks	375 mL
1 cup	sliced carrots	250 mL
1 cup	chopped green or yellow peppers	250 mL
3/4 cup	sliced zucchini	175 mL
1/4 cup	tomato paste	50 mL
1/3 cup	red or white wine	75 mL
2 cups	chopped tomatoes	500 mL
2 cups	beef or chicken stock	500 mL
2 tsp	dried rosemary	10 mL
1	bay leaf	1

Mashed Potatoes

1 1/2 lbs	potatoes, peeled and quartered	750 g
1 tbsp	margarine or butter	15 mL
1 tbsp	minced garlic	15 mL
1 cup	chopped onion	250 mL
1/2 cup	chicken stock	125 mL
1/3 cup	light sour cream	75 mL
1/4 tsp	ground black pepper	1 mL

1. In large nonstick saucepan, heat 2 tsp (10 mL) of the oil over medium-high heat. Dust the lamb cubes in the flour and add to the saucepan. Cook for 5 minutes or until well-browned on all sides. Remove lamb from saucepan.

2. Blanch the pearl onions in a pot of boiling water for 1 minute; refresh in cold water and drain. Peel and set aside.

3. In same saucepan, heat remaining 1 tsp (5 mL) oil over medium heat; add garlic, mushrooms, leeks, carrots, green peppers, zucchini and pearl onions. Cook for 8 to 10 minutes or until softened and browned, stirring occasionally. Stir in tomato paste and wine.

Return lamb to saucepan along with tomatoes, beef stock, rosemary and bay leaf. Bring to a boil, cover, reduce heat to medium-low, and simmer for 25 minutes or until carrots and meat are tender.

4. Meanwhile, put potatoes in a saucepan with water to cover; bring to a boil and cook for 15 minutes or until tender when pierced with the tip of a knife. In nonstick skillet, melt margarine over medium heat; add garlic and onions and cook for 4 minutes or until softened. Drain cooked potatoes and mash with chicken stock and sour cream. Stir in onion mixture and pepper. Place potato mixture on large serving platter and pour stew over top.

Serves 4

Curried Lamb Casserole with Sweet Potatoes

TIP

Other vegetables can be used in this recipe.

•

Adjust the curry powder to your taste.

•

Serve over rice, linguine or couscous.

MAKE AHEAD

Make and refrigerate up to a day ahead and reheat on low heat. This dish can also be frozen.

3/4 lb	lamb, cut into 3/4-inch (2 cm) cubes	375 g
	All-purpose flour for dusting	
1 tbsp	vegetable oil	15 mL
2 tsp	crushed garlic	10 mL
1 cup	chopped onion	250 mL
1 cup	finely chopped carrots	250 mL
1/2 cup	finely chopped sweet green pepper	125 mL
1 cup	cubed peeled sweet potatoes	250 mL
1 1/2 cups	sliced mushrooms	375 mL
2 1/2 cups	beef stock	625 mL
1/3 cup	red wine	75 mL
3 tbsp	tomato paste	45 mL
2 tsp	curry powder	10 mL

1. Dust lamb with flour.

2. In large nonstick Dutch oven, heat oil, sauté lamb for 2 minutes or just until seared all over. Remove lamb and set aside.

3. To skillet, add garlic, onion, carrots, green pepper and sweet potatoes; cook, stirring often, for 8 to 10 minutes or until tender. Add mushrooms and cook until softened, approximately 3 minutes.

4. Add stock, wine, tomato paste and curry powder. Return lamb to pan; cover and simmer for 1 1/2 hours, stirring occasionally.

FROM

Rose Reisman Brings Home Light Cooking

Serves 4

TIP

For a different version, try beef or lamb and other vegetables.

The longer the veal stews, the more tender the meat.

MAKE AHEAD

Prepare up to a day before and refrigerate, or freeze for longer storage. Reheat gently on a low heat.

FROM
Rose Reisman Brings Home Light Cooking

Veal Stew in Chunky Tomato Sauce

1 lb	boneless stewing veal, cut into 1-inch (2.5 cm) cubes	500 g
	All-purpose flour for dusting	
1 tbsp	vegetable oil	15 mL
2 tsp	crushed garlic	10 mL
1 cup	chopped onions	250 mL
1/2 cup	chopped sweet green pepper	125 mL
1 cup	chopped carrots	250 mL
1 1/2 cups	sliced mushrooms	375 mL
1 1/2 cups	beef stock	375 mL
1	bay leaf	1
1 tsp	dried oregano	5 mL
1 1/2 tsp	dried basil (or 2 tbsp [25 mL] chopped fresh)	7 mL
1 cup	chopped peeled potato	250 mL
1 cup	tomato sauce	250 mL
2 tbsp	tomato paste	25 mL
1/4 cup	red wine	50 mL

1. Dust veal cubes in flour.

2. In large nonstick Dutch oven, heat oil; sauté veal for 2 minutes. Remove veal and set aside.

3. To pan, add garlic, onions, green pepper, carrots and mushrooms; sauté until softened, approximately 5 minutes.

4. Add stock, bay leaf, oregano, basil, potato, tomato sauce, tomato paste and wine. Return veal to pan; cover and simmer for 1 hour or until veal is tender, stirring occasionally. Discard bay leaf.

Fish & Seafood Stews

Serves 4 to 5

I was served this wonderful seafood and rice dish at a catered outdoor 20-course seafood banquet at the seaside cottage of an old wealthy Taiwanese family into which an American university classmate of mine had married; she was fluent in Japanese and used that colonial tongue to converse with her in-laws.

Here I saw the deep impression the 75-year Japanese occupation of the Chinese island had made in Taiwanese culture and food. Japanese seafood preparations were followed by Chinese soups and native Taiwanese cooking, with its lavish use of basil and chilies. The meal ended with this rice dish. The juices of the seafood mingle deliciously with the seasoned sticky rice base. It's an exciting and elegant party dish that could be preceded by a clear soup or simple appetizer and accompanied by one or two vegetable side dishes.

FROM
The Asian Bistro Cookbook by Andrew Chase

Taiwanese Seafood Paella

2 cups	sticky rice	500 mL
3 tbsp	rice vinegar	45 mL
2 tbsp	fine ginger root julienne	25 mL
2	thinly sliced finger chilies	2
2 tbsp	soya sauce	25 mL
1 tbsp	lemon juice	15 mL
1 tsp	minced garlic	5 mL
12	dried black mushrooms (shiitake)	12
4 tsp	dried shrimp	20 mL
1/2 cup	vegetable oil	125 mL
1/3 cup	thinly sliced shallots	75 mL
1 tsp	minced ginger root	5 mL
1 tbsp	Chinese rice wine *or* dry sherry or *sake*	15 mL
8 to 10 oz	large shrimps	250 to 375 g
24	clams or mussels	24
2	squid, cleaned	2
1 3/4 cups	chicken stock	425 mL
1/2 cup	green onion rings	125 mL
1/2 tsp	salt	2 mL
1	1 1/2 to 2 lbs (750 g to 1 kg) lobster *or* 1 to 2 crabs	1

1. Soak sticky rice in 4 cups (1 L) water for 6 to 8 hours.
2. Prepare two simple dipping sauces: In a small saucer, combine rice vinegar and ginger julienne; in another saucer, stir together chilies, soya sauce, lemon juice and garlic. Set sauces aside.
3. Cover mushrooms in cold water and soak 10 minutes or until soft. Drain, discarding liquid. Remove and discard stems; quarter mushroom caps and set aside. Soak dried shrimp in cold water to cover for 10 minutes; drain and set aside. In a saucepan heat oil over medium-high heat; cook shallots until golden. Strain, reserving oil; set shallots aside. In 2 tbsp (25 mL) of the shallot oil cook dried shrimp and ginger over medium-high heat for 30 seconds; stir in mushrooms and cook until browned. Stir in wine; cook until liquid evaporates. Set aside.

continued on page 70

4. Cut legs off shrimp with scissors but keep shells on; devein. Rinse clams or rinse and debeard the mussels. Cut the squid tubes into rings and separate the tentacles into 2 or 3 sections. (Or cut in the Chinese fashion: Cut open the tubes, lay them on the board exterior-side down and score a close crisscross pattern into, but not completely through, the interior flesh; cut diagonally into strips.)

5. Drain rice; in a shallow casserole dish, carefully mix rice with shallots, mushroom mixture, stock, green onions and salt without browning the rice kernels. Bring to a simmer on the stove, cover well and place in preheated 350° F (180° C) oven. Cook 30 minutes

6. Meanwhile, prepare lobster or crab. For lobster: pull off claws, divide into 2 sections and crack shells lightly with side of knife; cut tail from body and divide horizontally into 3 sections or split lengthwise; divide body lengthwise into 2 pieces (carefully preserving the tamale and roe). For crab: Remove claws and crack; lift off flap from bottom shell and discard; with a knife or cleaver, carefully pry off the back shell from the body and retain shell with any roe; divide the body in half lengthwise through the middle (discarding the white heart and innards between the two halves), remove the lungs from the outside of each half and cut each half into 2 pieces (2 legs each).

7. After rice has cooked 30 minutes, put lobster or crab on top of rice; cover and cook 12 minutes longer. Add shrimp and clams or mussels; cover and cook 5 minutes. Add squid; cover and cook 5 minutes longer. Serve with dipping sauces on the side.

Cod Provençal

What to do with fresh cod from the market and ripe tomatoes plucked from your garden? Add some briny olives and pungent capers, and make this delicious fish dish that bursts with the sunny flavors of the Mediterranean.

TIP

Don't skimp on the olive oil — it's what gives this dish its distinct character and flavor.

PREHEAT OVEN TO 425° F (220° C)
SHALLOW BAKING DISH

1 1/4 lbs	cod or halibut, cut into 4 pieces	625 g
	Salt and pepper	
2	ripe tomatoes, diced	2
2	green onions	2
1	clove garlic, minced	1
1/4 cup	Kalamata olives, rinsed, cut into slivers	50 mL
2 tbsp	chopped fresh parsley or basil	25 mL
1 tbsp	capers, rinsed and drained	15 mL
Pinch	red pepper flakes (optional)	Pinch
2 tbsp	olive oil	25 mL

1. Arrange cod in a single layer in baking dish. Season with salt and pepper.

2. In a bowl combine tomatoes, onions, garlic, olives, parsley, capers and hot pepper flakes, if using; season with salt and pepper. Spoon tomato-olive mixture over fish fillets; drizzle with oil.

3. Bake in preheated oven for 15 to 20 minutes or until fish flakes when tested with a fork. Serve in warmed wide shallow bowls and spoon pan juices over.

FROM
**The Comfort Food Cookbook
by Johanna Burkhard**

Thai Shrimp Curry with Pineapple and Squash

Serves 4

Lobster or crab is delicious cooked in this curry sauce. Instead of shrimp, add cut-up lobsters or crabs in their shells to the sauce at the same time as the squash and pineapple. The shrimp stock is unnecessary.
If you live in an area with Thai grocers, then add 1 finely sliced wild ginger tuber (gachai or kratchai) while frying the curry paste and, if desired, add 3 deveined lime leaves with the shrimp.
This is an unusual and delicious Thai curry. Massaman curry paste is from the Muslim south of Thailand and is sometimes available in small tins at Asian grocers. Thai red curry paste is more widely available and can be used here with the addition of a few spices. It is slightly hotter than massaman paste so you might want to reduce the amount a little for a milder curry.
For extra heat, serve with small saucers of ground dry-roasted chilies to sprinkle over the curry (roast small dried red chilies in a dry pan over medium heat until slightly browned, then grind or pound to a powder) or with chopped bird-eye chilies soaked in a little fish sauce and a squirt of lime juice. Like all Thai curries, this one should be served with lots of white rice, preferably fragrant rice (sometimes called "jasmine rice" or "scented rice") from Thailand.

FROM
The Asian Bistro Cookbook by Andrew Chase

1 lb	shrimp, unshelled	500 g
Half	onion, sliced	Half
1	stalk coriander (with roots)	1
10	black peppercorns	10
5	slices ginger root	5
1/2 tsp	salt	2 mL
2 tsp	vegetable oil	10 mL
4 tsp	Thai massaman curry paste *or* red curry paste with 1/8 tsp (0.5 mL) each ground cinnamon, cardamom and nutmeg	20 mL
1	stalk lemon grass, cut into short lengths	1
1 tsp	palm sugar *or* light brown sugar	10 mL
1 tbsp	ground dry-roasted peanuts	15 mL
1	can (14 oz [400 mL]) coconut milk	1
2 tsp	fish sauce *or* 3/4 tsp (4 mL) salt	10 mL
3/4 cup	calabasa squash *or* orange-fleshed squash (such as acorn, pumpkin, butternut), cut into bite-size pieces	175 mL
3/4 cup	pineapple, cut into bite-size pieces	175 mL
1/4 cup	coriander sprigs	50 mL

1. Peel and devein shrimp, reserving shells. In a small saucepan, combine shells, onion, coriander, peppercorns, ginger, salt and 3/4 cup (175 mL) water. Bring to a boil, reduce heat to low, cover and cook 20 minutes. Strain, discarding solids; set aside.

2. In a saucepan, heat oil over medium heat; cook curry paste and lemon grass, stirring, until fragrant. Stir in sugar and 2 tsp (10 mL) of the peanuts; cook, stirring, 10 to 20 seconds. Gradually stir in coconut milk, fish sauce and shrimp stock; bring to a boil, reduce heat to low and cook 5 minutes. (Recipe can be prepared to this point several hours ahead of time.)

3. Bring sauce to a simmer over medium heat. Stir in squash and pineapple, cover and cook 4 minutes or until squash is almost tender. Stir in shrimp, cover and cook 2 to 3 minutes or until cooked through. Serve garnished with coriander and sprinkled with remaining ground peanuts.

Serves 4

Paella Rodriguez

It's hard to say which came first, paella or risotto. Similar as they are in method, however, the end results define — in culinary terms, at least — the essential difference between the Spanish and the Italians. What is basically a flavorful, savory porridge in the Italian kitchen becomes, in its Spanish counterpart, a fiesta of colors and diverse tastes.

Paella derives its primary signatures from chorizo (Spanish sausage), saffron and short-grain rice.

There are no truly exact measurements in paella and also no absolutely exact times. This recipe, created by writer and good friend Juan Rodriguez, can be followed to the letter, but as you will see there are moments when you'll have to be the boss: Decide when to stir, when to reduce or increase heat, whether it could use an extra

continued on page 76

PREHEAT OVEN TO 350° F (180° C)

1 lb	chicken drumsticks (about 4)	500 g
6 oz	chorizo sausage	150 g
1/3 cup	olive oil	75 mL
2 cups	finely diced onions	500 mL
1	green pepper, cut into 1/2-inch (1 cm) squares	1
Half	red bell pepper, cut into 1/2-inch (1 cm) squares	Half
5	cloves garlic, chopped	5
2 cups	short-grain rice	500 mL
1 tsp	saffron threads, crumbled	5 mL
3/4 cup	frozen peas	175 mL
6 cups	boiling medium-strength salted chicken stock	1.5 L
1/2 cup	white wine	125 mL
1/2 cup	clam juice *or* 1/2 cup (125 mL) additional white wine	125 mL
8 oz	cleaned squid, cut into 1/4-inch (5 mm) rings	250 g
8 oz	clams or mussels	250 g
1	medium tomato, seeded and cut into 1/2-inch (1 cm) cubes	1
3 tbsp	lemon juice	45 mL
8 oz	raw shrimp, peeled and deveined	250 g
4	canned artichoke hearts, drained and cut in half	4
	Lemon wedges	
	Salt and pepper to taste	

1. Bake chicken drumsticks to almost-but-not-quite done, about 30 minutes. Set aside. Meanwhile, slice chorizo in 1/4-inch (5 mm) rings and cut rings in half to get half-moon pieces. In a frying pan, heat 1 tsp (5 mL) of the olive oil over high heat; add chorizo and cook, stirring often, for 3 minutes or until cooked but before it chars. With a slotted spoon, remove chorizo; set aside. Discard rendered chorizo fat.

continued on page 76

Continued from page 75

measure of stock; to let it catch a little to the pan (very tasty), but stop cooking before anything actually burns (bitter and unpleasant). Possibly the biggest variable is the kind of pan one uses. A metal pan will conduct heat better and is traditional, but the non-stick type we recommend is safer as it is less likely to burn the rice. When you've put up with all its quirks and mastered it, paella is extremely rewarding. It is as terrific for intimate dinners, as it is for larger affairs, and leftovers are excellent the next day. We suggest you try this recipe for 4 to get the hang of it and then multiply the quantities for a large celebratory batch with your friends.

2. In a deep nonstick saucepan, heat remaining olive oil over high heat for 1 minute. Add onions, green and red pepper; cook, stirring, for 2 minutes. Reduce heat to medium-high; cook, stirring often, about 8 minutes or until softened, golden, reduced in volume and just beginning to char. Add garlic and sauté 1 minute. Reduce heat to low. Add rice and saffron; cook, stirring, until well coated with oil. Stir in peas and chorizo.

3. Now begins the addition of the liquid and a cooking process of about 40 minutes. It is important to let each addition be absorbed before adding the next, and to keep playing with the heat, so that there is constant bubbling (keep your stock boiling as you use it). Start by stirring in 2 cups (500 mL) of the chicken stock. Raise heat to medium-high. Cook, stirring, for 5 to 6 minutes; as the liquid is absorbed, add wine and clam juice. Cook, stirring, 2 to 3 minutes or until absorbed.

4. Add 1/2 cup (125 mL) of stock and the squid. Cook, stirring, 2 minutes or until absorbed. Add another 1/2 cup (125 mL) stock, the clams and chicken drumsticks. Cook, stirring, 2 to 4 minutes or until absorbed. Stir in tomato. Add stock in increments of 1/2 cup (125 mL) and keep cooking and stirring to absorb each addition for 2 to 4 minutes before adding the next. Test your rice before adding the final half cups of stock. It should be soft but still separate, and the paella should be glistening, a little saucy and beginning to catch a touch on the bottom of the pan. Ideally you will have 1/2 cup (125 mL) of stock left over.

5. Reduce heat to medium-low. Sprinkle evenly with lemon juice; mix in. Stir in shrimp and place artichoke hearts on top of the rice. Cook undisturbed for 1 minute. Take off heat and cover loosely. Let rest for 15 minutes to develop flavor and absorb liquids.

6. Present paella in its cooking pot and let people serve themselves. Pass lemon wedges, salt and pepper for individual seasoning. Accompany with crusty bread and a green salad.

Serves 4

Shrimp and Scallops with Cheesy Cream Sauce

TIP

Other firm white fish such as grouper, cod or halibut can be cut into chunks, to substitute for the seafood.

Freeze shrimp with their shells to preserve the best taste.

1 tbsp	margarine	15 mL
1 tsp	crushed garlic	5 mL
1/3 cup	chopped green onions	75 mL
1 lb	seafood (shrimp, scallops or combination)	500 g
1/4 cup	chopped fresh parsley	50 mL
2 oz	goat or feta cheese, crumbled	50 g

Sauce

1 tbsp	margarine	15 mL
2 1/2 tsp	all-purpose flour	12 mL
1/3 cup	dry white wine	75 mL
1/2 cup	2% milk	125 mL

1. Sauce: In small saucepan, melt margarine; stir in flour and cook, stirring, for 1 minute. Add wine and milk; cook, stirring, until thickened and smooth, approximately 2 minutes. Set aside and keep warm.

2. In nonstick skillet, melt margarine; sauté garlic, green onions and seafood just until seafood is opaque. Remove from stove; add sauce and mix well.

3. Pour into serving dish; sprinkle parsley and cheese over top.

FROM
Rose Reisman Brings Home Light Cooking

FROM
Rose Reisman Brings Home Light Cooking

Seafood Tomato Stew

Serves 6

TIP

Known as a cioppino, this seafood dish can be made with any combination of seafood. Other chopped vegetables can also be added.

•

Serve with French or Italian bread.

MAKE AHEAD

Follow steps 1 to 3 early in day. Later, reheat the sauce, then add seafood and cook as directed.

1 tbsp	vegetable oil	15 mL
Half	medium onion, chopped	Half
Half	celery stalk, chopped	Half
1 tsp	crushed garlic	5 mL
1/4 lb	mushrooms, sliced	125 g
2	cans (each 19 oz [540 mL]) tomatoes, crushed	2
2 tbsp	tomato paste	25 mL
1/3 cup	white wine *or* fish stock	75 mL
1 1/2 tsp	dried oregano	7 mL
1 1/2 tsp	dried basil	7 mL
24	mussels	24
1/2 lb	shrimp, peeled and deveined	250 g
1/2 lb	scallops	250 g
1/2 lb	firm white fish (cod, halibut, haddock), cut into bite-sized pieces	250 g
	Chopped fresh parsley	

1. In large nonstick saucepan, heat oil; sauté onion, celery, garlic and mushrooms until softened, approximately 5 minutes.

2. Add tomatoes, tomato paste, wine, oregano, basil and bay leaves; cover and simmer for 25 minutes, stirring occasionally.

3. Scrub mussels under cold water; remove any beards. Discard any that do not close when tapped.

4. Add mussels, shrimp, scallops and fish to pot; cover and cook for 5 to 8 minutes or until mussels open, shrimp are pink and scallops and fish are opaque. Discard any mussels that do not open. Discard bay leaves. Serve immediately.

Mussels with Pesto

Serves 4

Pesto

1 1/4 cups	packed fresh basil	300 mL
3 tbsp	olive oil	45 mL
2 tbsp	toasted pine nuts	25 mL
2 tbsp	grated Parmesan cheese	25 mL
1 tsp	minced garlic	5 mL
1/4 cup	chicken stock	50 mL
1/4 cup	white wine *or* chicken stock	50 mL
2 lbs	cleaned mussels	1 kg

1. Pesto: Put basil, olive oil, pine nuts, Parmesan and garlic in food processor; process until finely chopped, scraping down sides of bowl once. With machine running, gradually add stock through feed tube; process until smooth.

2. Put pesto and wine in large heavy-bottomed saucepan. Bring to a boil; add mussels and cover. Cook, shaking the saucepan for 2 minutes, or just until mussels open. Discard any that do not open.

TIP

To clean mussels, cut off any beards that are visible and check condition of mussels' shells — discard any with cracked or broken shells, as well as any that are opened and will not close when you tap them.

•

If basil is unavailable, use parsley or a combination.

•

Try clams instead of mussels.

•

Use french bread to soak up sauce.

MAKE AHEAD

Prepare pesto earlier in the day, cover and refrigerate. Pesto can also be frozen for up to 2 weeks.

FROM
**Rose Reisman's Enlightened
Home Cooking**

Asian Seafood and Tomato Stew

Serves 4

In this recipe, the classic combination of tomato and garlic is enlivened with horseradish and toasted chili oil. The seafood is lightly poached in the hot broth and will cook very quickly.

This is great over steamed rice.

FROM
**New World Chinese Cooking
by Bill Jones and
Stephen Wong**

PREHEAT OVEN TO 350° F (180° C)

4 cups	tomato juice	1 L
2 cups	chicken stock	500 mL
1 tbsp	minced garlic	15 mL
1 tbsp	minced ginger root	15 mL
2 tbsp	honey	25 mL
1	medium onion, thinly sliced	1
2 tbsp	horseradish	25 mL
1	red bell pepper, seeded and finely diced	1
12 oz	seafood (shrimp, peeled and deveined, and/or scallops)	375 g
1 lb	mussels and/or clams	500 g
1 cup	shredded bok choy	250 mL
2 tbsp	cornstarch dissolved in 4 tbsp (60 mL) water	25 mL
1 tbsp	minced cilantro	15 mL
1 tbsp	TOASTED CHILI OIL (see recipe, page 82)	15 mL
	Salt and pepper to taste	

1. In a medium saucepan, combine tomato juice, chicken stock, garlic, ginger root, honey, onion, horseradish and red bell pepper. Bring to a boil. Reduce heat and simmer for 20 minutes.

2. Add seafood, mussels or clams and bok choy; simmer until seafood is tender and all shells have opened (discard those that fail to open after 5 minutes). Add dissolved cornstarch; stir until mixture thickens. Season with cilantro, chili oil, salt and pepper. Serve immediately.

**Makes about
2 cups (500 mL)**

Toasted Chili Oil

*Although chili peppers
were unknown in China
for much of its history
(they were imported
from Central America
only a few hundred
years ago), chili oil
is now a staple
ingredient in
Chinese cooking.*

*This oil has a more
pungent, smoky flavor
than commercially
available varieties.*

*The oil will keep up to
2 months in the
refrigerator.*

| 2 tbsp | dried chili flakes | 25 mL |
| 2 cups | vegetable oil | 500 mL |

1. In a heavy skillet or small saucepan, heat chili flakes until toasted and almost smoking. Carefully pour in the oil and heat for 1 minute. Remove from heat and allow the flavors to infuse for at least 20 minutes.

2. Transfer to a sterilized glass jar or bottle and refrigerate.

FROM
**New World Chinese Cooking
by Bill Jones and
Stephen Wong**

Vegetable Stews

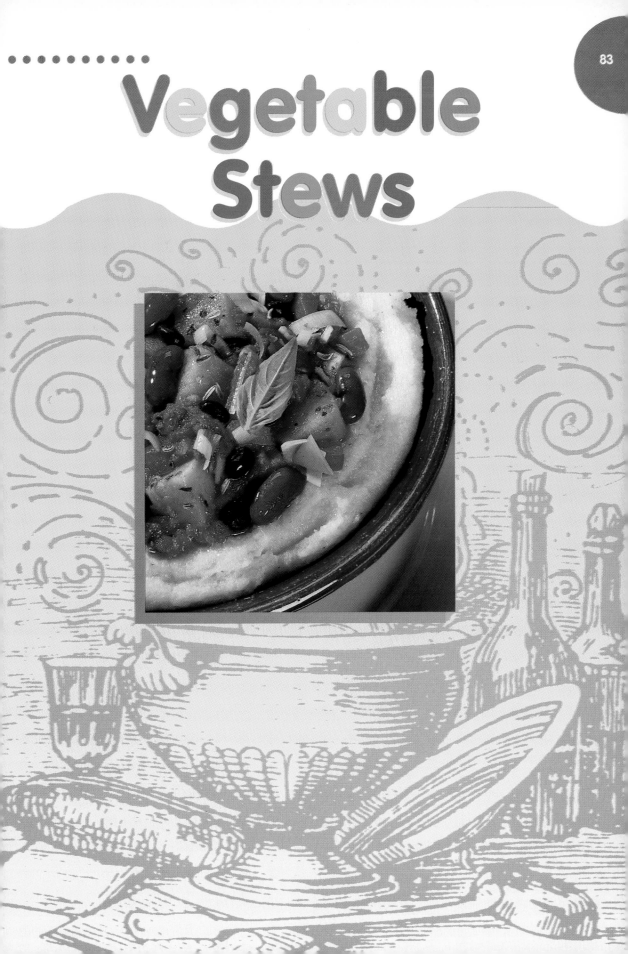

Serves 6

Bean and Sweet Potato Chili on Garlic Polenta

TIP

Use any cooked beans that you have on hand.

Try fresh fennel instead of leeks.

Polenta is delicious, nutritious and takes minutes to make.

A great source of fiber.

MAKE AHEAD

Prepare chili up to 2 days in advance. Cook polenta just before serving.

FROM
Rose Reisman's Light Vegetarian Cooking

Chili

2 tsp	vegetable oil	10 mL
1 1/2 tsp	minced garlic	7 mL
1 1/2 cups	chopped leeks	375 mL
1 cup	chopped red bell peppers	250 mL
1	can (19 oz [540 mL]) tomatoes, puréed	1
1 1/2 cups	canned red kidney beans, rinsed and drained	375 mL
1 1/4 cups	chopped peeled sweet potatoes	300 mL
1 tbsp	fennel seeds	15 mL
2 tsp	chili powder	10 mL
1 tsp	dried basil	5 mL

Polenta

3 1/4 cups	vegetable stock	800 mL
1 cup	cornmeal	250 mL
1 tsp	minced garlic	5 mL

1. In a large nonstick saucepan, heat oil over medium–high heat. Add garlic, leeks and red peppers; cook 4 minutes or until softened. Stir in tomatoes, beans, sweet potatoes, fennel seeds, chili powder and basil; bring to a boil. Reduce heat to medium-low, cover and cook 20 to 25 minutes or until sweet potatoes are tender.

2. Meanwhile, in a deep saucepan, bring vegetable stock to a boil. Reduce heat to low and gradually whisk in cornmeal and garlic. Cook 5 minutes, stirring frequently.

3. Pour polenta into a serving dish. Spoon chili over top. Serve immediately.

Chickpea Tofu Stew

Serves 4

A filling and flavorful winter dish, this stew is bolstered with the addition of the super-nutritious tofu. It is imperative to use firm tofu (often called "pressed tofu"), since the soft variety will disintegrate. For chickpeas, you can either cook your own, or use the canned variety.

Excellent served with a salad, steamed rice and a yogurt-based sauce.

For a spicier flavor, substitute cayenne pepper for the chili powder.

FROM
**The New Vegetarian Gourmet
by Byron Ayanoglu**

PREHEAT OVEN TO 375° F (190° C)
6-CUP (1.5 L) CASSEROLE DISH

1 lb	ripe tomatoes (about 4)	500 g
3 tbsp	olive oil	45 mL
1/2 tsp	salt	2 mL
1/2 tsp	paprika	2 mL
1/2 tsp	whole cumin seeds	2 mL
1/2 tsp	chili powder	2 mL
2 1/2 cups	thinly sliced onions	625 mL
1/2	green pepper, thinly sliced	1/2
4	cloves garlic, thinly sliced	4
2	bay leaves	2
1 cup	hot water	250 mL
2 tsp	lime juice	10 mL
2 cups	cooked chickpeas	500 mL
1/2 lb	firm tofu, cut into 1/2-inch (1 cm) cubes	250 g
1 tsp	olive oil (optional)	5 mL
1/4 cup	finely diced red onions	50 mL
	Few sprigs fresh coriander, chopped	

1. Blanch tomatoes in boiling water for 30 seconds. Over a bowl, peel, core and deseed them. Chop tomatoes into chunks and set aside. Strain any accumulated tomato juices from bowl; add the juices to the tomatoes.

2. In a large frying pan, heat olive oil over high heat for 30 seconds. Add salt, paprika, cumin seeds and chili powder in quick succession. Stir-fry for 30 seconds. Add onions and stir-fry for 1 minute. Add green peppers and stir-fry for 2 to 3 minutes, until soft. Add garlic and stir-fry for 1 minute. Add the tomato flesh and juices. Stir-cook for 3 minutes to break up the tomato somewhat. Add the bay leaves, hot water and lime juice. Cook, stirring often, for 5 minutes.

3. Transfer sauce to casserole dish. Fold the chickpeas into the sauce. Distribute the tofu cubes evenly over the surface, and gently press them down into the sauce.

4. Bake the stew, uncovered, for 25 to 30 minutes, until bubbling and bright. Drizzle with olive oil (if using) and garnish with red onions and coriander.

Creamy Eggplant Zucchini Moussaka

Serves 6

TIP

Leaving the skin on vegetables increases the fiber.

•

Replace feta with goat cheese, Cheddar or another strong-tasting cheese.

•

Great reheated the next day.

MAKE AHEAD

Prepare vegetable mixture and milk sauce early in the day. Assemble and bake just before serving.

FROM
Rose Reisman's Enlightened Home Cooking

PREHEAT OVEN TO 350° F (180° C)
8-INCH (2 L) SQUARE BAKING DISH

2 tsp	vegetable oil	10 mL
2 tsp	minced garlic	10 mL
1 3/4 cups	chopped onions	425 mL
1 3/4 cups	unpeeled zucchini cut into 1/2-inch (1 cm) cubes	425 mL
1 3/4 cups	unpeeled eggplant cut into 1/2-inch (1 cm) cubes	425 mL
1 3/4 cups	sliced mushrooms	425 mL
1 1/2 tsp	dried basil	7 mL
1 tsp	dried oregano	5 mL
2 tsp	margarine or butter	10 mL
1 tbsp	flour	15 mL
1 cup	2% milk	250 mL
1	egg	1
1 cup	5% ricotta cheese	250 mL
1 cup	tomato pasta sauce	250 mL
3 oz	feta cheese, crumbled	75 g

1. In nonstick skillet sprayed with vegetable spray, heat oil over medium heat. Cook garlic, onions, zucchini and eggplant for 10 minutes or until softened, stirring occasionally. Add mushrooms, basil and oregano and cook for 4 minutes longer, or until vegetables are tender.

2. In small saucepan, melt margarine over medium heat; add flour and cook, stirring, for 1 minute. Gradually add milk and cook, stirring, for 4 minutes or until sauce begins to simmer. Remove from heat and let cool for 5 minutes. Whisk in egg and ricotta.

3.. Spread tomato sauce over bottom of baking dish. Add vegetable mixture and top with milk sauce. Sprinkle with crumbled feta. Bake uncovered for 20 minutes or until heated through, and edges are set. Let rest 5 minutes before serving.

Pumpkin and Lotus Root Stew

Serves 4

5	large dried Chinese black mushrooms	5
2	strips bacon, chopped	2
1 tbsp	chopped shallots	15 mL
1 tsp	minced garlic	5 mL
3 cups	pumpkin or squash flesh cut into 1-inch (2.5 cm) cubes	750 mL
1	6-inch (15 cm) piece lotus root *or* 4-inch (10 cm) length daikon radish, cut crosswise into 1/4-inch (5 mm) thick slices	1
1 cup	chicken stock	250 mL
1 tbsp	dark soya sauce	15 mL
1 tbsp	oyster sauce	15 mL
2	green onions, cut into 2-inch (5 cm) lengths	2
1 tbsp	cornstarch dissolved in mushroom liquid	15 mL
	Salt and pepper to taste	

Practically every part of the lotus plant is used in China: The flower is admired for its beauty; the leaves are used for wrapping food; the seeds are made into a sweet filling for desserts; and the lotus root is used in stews and stir-fries. Many western chefs have now taken to slicing the dramatic look-ing root into paper-thin slices and deep-frying them to use as a garnish.

While buying lotus roots, look for those that are plump, heavy, beige in color and free of blemishes.

FROM
New World Chinese Cooking by Bill Jones and Stephen Wong

1. In a heatproof bowl, soak mushrooms in 1/2 cup (125 mL) boiling water for 15 minutes. Drain and reserve liquid. Remove stems; slice caps diagonally in half and set aside.

2. Heat a wok or deep skillet over medium heat. Add bacon and fry until golden and slightly crisp, about 2 minutes. Drain all but 1 tbsp (15 mL) fat from wok. Add shallots, garlic, mushrooms, pumpkin and lotus root; sauté for 2 minutes. Add stock, soya sauce and oyster sauce; bring to a boil. Cover and cook 10 minutes or until vegetables are tender. Add green onions; stir to mix and cook 1 minute. Stir in dissolved cornstarch; bring to a boil and cook until sauce is slightly thickened. Season with salt and pepper. Serve.

Serves 6

TIP

The darker the skin of the sweet potato, the moister it is.

Sweet potatoes are sweet on their own. Lessen the honey or maple syrup if desired.

Chopped dates or apricots can replace the raisins.

MAKE AHEAD

Prepare casserole without apples up to the day before. Add apples, toss and bake just prior to serving.

FROM
**Rose Reisman Brings Home
Light Cooking**

Sweet Potato, Apple and Raisin Casserole

PREHEAT OVEN TO 350° F (180° C)
BAKING DISH SPRAYED WITH NONSTICK VEGETABLE SPRAY

1 lb	sweet potatoes, peeled and cubed	500 g
3/4 tsp	ground ginger	4 mL
1/4 cup	honey *or* maple syrup	50 mL
3/4 tsp	ground cinnamon	4 mL
2 tbsp	margarine, melted	25 mL
1/4 cup	raisins	50 mL
2 tbsp	chopped walnuts	25 mL
3/4 cup	cubed peeled sweet apples	175 mL

1. Steam or microwave sweet potatoes just until slightly underdone. Drain and place in baking dish.

2. In a small bowl, combine ginger, honey, cinnamon, margarine, raisins, walnuts and apples; mix well. Pour over sweet potatoes and bake, uncovered, for 20 minutes or until tender.

Cheesy Ratatouille Bean Casserole

Serves 4 or 5

TIP

Any beans can be used. Try red or white kidney beans, chickpeas or navy beans.

Other vegetables such as sweet peppers, parsnips or carrots can be substituted.

For extra fiber, leave on the skin of the zucchini and eggplant.

MAKE AHEAD

Prepare and refrigerate up to a day before and bake just before serving. This is delicious reheated.

PREHEAT OVEN TO 400° F (200° C)

1 tbsp	vegetable oil	15 mL
2 tsp	crushed garlic	10 mL
1	medium onion, diced	1
1 cup	sliced mushrooms	250 mL
1 cup	thickly sliced zucchini	250 mL
2 cups	cubed eggplant	500 mL
1 cup	cubed peeled potatoes	250 mL
1	can (19 oz [540 mL]) tomatoes, crushed	1
1 cup	drained cooked beans	250 mL
1 tsp	dried oregano	5 mL
1 tsp	dried basil	5 mL
1 cup	shredded mozzarella cheese	250 mL

1. In a large nonstick saucepan, heat oil over medium heat; cook garlic, onion, mushrooms, zucchini and eggplant, stirring constantly, for about 10 minutes or until softened.

2. Add potatoes, tomatoes, beans, oregano and basil; simmer for 30 minutes or until potatoes are tender.

3. Pour into large baking dish and sprinkle with mozzarella. Bake for 10 minutes or until cheese melts.

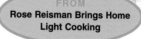

FROM
Rose Reisman Brings Home Light Cooking

Index

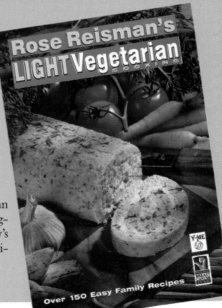

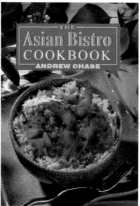